WE'RE FROM DUFFIELD

by

STAN PERKINS

So that you will know and remember us in Duffield

Stan Perkins

BROADBLADE PRESS
11314 Miller Road
Swartz Creek, MI 48473

DUFFIELD CHURCH
Duffield Community Methodist Church as of April 20, 1982

Dedicated to
The Pioneer Families that settled the
Duffield Community

The life span of Duffield has been a grain of sand in the hourglass of the ages.

ISBN 0-9614640-1-1 (Casebound)
    0-9614640-2-X (Paperback)

Copyright © 1982 by Stan Perkins
Second Edition 1985

All rights reserved. No part of this book shall be reproduced in any form or transmitted by any electronic or mechanical means, including photocopying, recording, and information retrieval system, without written permission from the Publisher.

Typeset and printed in the United States of America by
Sans Serif, Inc., and McNaughton & Gunn.

CONTENTS

ILLUSTRATIONS vi
ACKNOWLEDGEMENTS viii
PROLOGUE ix

CHAPTER I
    COMMUNITY NAMESAKE 1
CHAPTER II
    THE CHURCH 5
CHAPTER III
    THE DUFFIELD LADIES AID SOCIETY 15
CHAPTER IV
    THE FIRE 25
CHAPTER V
    YOUNG PEOPLE 37
CHAPTER VI
    THE RAILROAD 45
CHAPTER VII
    ONE ROOM SCHOOLS 57
CHAPTER VIII
    VILLAGE AND ADJACENT BUSINESSES 67
CHAPTER IX
    THE HUMAN SIDE 113
CHAPTER X
    PERSONALITIES AT LARGE 125
CHAPTER XI
    PATRIOTS AND WAR VETERANS 139
CHAPTER XII
    CONCLUSION 143
BIBLIOGRAPHY 147

ILLUSTRATIONS

The Duffield Church	ii
Portion of Michigan Road Map	xi
Edward Herrick Family and Pioneer Home	xii
Dr. Samuel Pearce Duffield	2
Duffield, Parke & Company Advertising	3
New Church as Constructed in 1891	4
Samuel W. Bird, Pastor, 1898-1902	13
The Duffield Church, 1899	14
The Church as Rebuilt	24
Bula and Evlyn Middlesworth	27
Merle Middlesworth and William Keeran	28
Mr. and Mrs. John Burns Admire Window	32
Up Goes the Spire	34
Church Chancel and Lloyd McLaren Family	36
Barefoots	39
All Dressed Up for Easter	40
Duffield Church Youth Group, May 1959	41
Agnes Jennings	43
First Railroad Survey Line 1869-70	46
Railroad Line as Constructed From Survey of 1876	47
Highballing Out of Duffield Station	50
Vanderbilt Depot	51
Depot for the Duration	52
The Essential Local Freight	53
The Steamer Engine 2681	54
The Steamer Engine 5632	54
Halpin School 1906	56
North Duffield School 1894	58
North Duffield School 1921	59
North Duffield School About 1926	60
Doane School in Session 1961	62
Doane School May 1911	65
Doane School 1924	66
A Corner of Gaines Township	68
The Hynes Ladies	69
Monthly Gleaner	70

The Middlesworth Factory	72
A Newfangled Windmill	74
Atherton's General Store	76
At the Depot With a Can of Cream	77
The New Store	78
Arthur Carrier, Country Merchant	80
The Merchant's Wife	80
The Institution, Rollin' Along	81
Col. Fenton C. Perkins	83
Maria Warner Carrier	85
Adelbert Carrier Family	85
Sugar Beets	88
Potato Digger	90
Duffield Farmers Elevator	92
Threshing Wheat With the Greyhound 20 H.P.	93
Reo Speedwagon Harnessed to Load of Hay	94
Restored Truck in Parade Form	95
Baling Hay Out of the Field	96
Three Generations Thresh With New Machine	98
First Prize Apples Genesee County Fair 1851	100
"And the Win-nah is, Goldenglo"	101
Carlos Domino 16 C.F. and His Keepers	102
Broadblade Farm Dispersal Auction 1948	103
Duffield People at Junior Livestock Show 1957	104
Grand Champion	105
A Fair Day	106
Melissa and Katrina	107
Champion Market Hog	108
New World's Champion Producer	109
Aerial View of Post & Sons Pit in Operation	110
Valley Farm Equipment	111
Asplin Cider Mill	112
The Lifeline	114
Traveling Salesman and Team	115
John and Ruth Burton on Their Wedding Day	122
Ben Hillaker and Brother	123
Mrs. Mina Hillaker and Daughter	124
Duell & Post and Their Farm Gate	128
Duffield Hillbilly Band	131
Receiving Their Masonic Degrees	133
Buzzing Wood With Steam Power	137
Fife Played in The War of 1812	138
Today's Bedroom Community South of Hill Road	142
Today's Bedroom Community North of Hill Road	142
A Duffield Landmark	145

ACKNOWLEDGEMENTS

William and Marguerite Ackerman
Howard Atherton
Patty Brisbane
Lyle and Delloise Buchanan
Beulah Burton
Emil Drlik
John and Beth Drlik
A. J. Ferguson, Jr.
Arlene Gabriz
Yutha Hayes
Eva Herrick
Agnes Jennings
Helen Lawrence
S. H. Maginity
Ardis McLaren
Marian Newman
George and Hila O'Brien
Brian Osmer
Ralph and Evelyn Parker
Naoma Perkins
Helen Perry
Harold and Beverly Post
Henry R. Robison
George Ryva
George and Elizabeth Stevenson
John D. Williams
Herthyl Withey
Harry and Marjorie Woods

And to many others for photos, for the accessibility to their family records and for their words of encouragement that have made "We're From Duffield" possible.

Edited by
Mary J. Shaw

PROLOGUE

THE INTENT OF THIS PUBLICATION is to preserve for posterity a record of the rise and fall of a typical midwestern community whose well-being paralleled that of the railroad and was based upon an agricultural economy. Presented are the history, happenings and bits of humor about Duffield, Michigan without becoming entangled in the genealogy of families. No punches have been pulled. On the contrary, it has been called like it is. There has been no effort to minimize the base or to maximize the virtue.

Illustrations and information, that compliment one another, have been provided by individuals whose names are listed under the acknowledgements. Additional information was gleaned from early maps, reference books and historical documents that are listed in the bibliography.

By an act of the Legislature on February 16, 1842 the area of Michigan that was previously identified as Mundy Township was divided into two equal parts with the western half being named Gaines Township for General Edmund T. Gaines, War of 1812. It was identifed as Township VI North Range V East.

According to statute, a township meeting was called for April 4th, 1842 with one Wm. Gazley appointed as moderator. "Of twenty-one eligible male voters who attended this meeting, sixteen were elected or appointed to at least one township office." Most of them lived near Fletchers Corner which is now the corner of Grand Blanc and Seymour Roads. The area that was to be known later as Duffield furnished the new township of Gaines its first supervisor. He was William B. Young who, together with his son, had taken up the west half of section 8 or 320 acres. The only other person, mentioned in the area covered by this writing, was Lyman Perkins from section 5 who was appointed to "Directors of the Poor." Martin Dart was elected clerk and Ephraim Fletcher, treasurer. It was voted to raise the sum of $80.00 for township expenses.

An early map charted on shellacked canvas, made by hand sometime after 1842 and before 1870, shows no through trails or roads across Gaines Township. The East-West Roads of some duration were Maple Avenue, Reid Road and Baldwin Road. The North-South Roads were less distinguishable with Seymour Road the most prominent. Along the survey line that was named Duffield Road, after Duffield Station in 1877, there was nothing. The same was true of the Genesee-Shiawassee County Line (Sheridan Avenue.) Swamps and other large undrained areas were the principal deterrent. Travel was by the long way around and followed the high land without objection from the landowners.

These low impassable stretches, along surveyed section lines, were corrected gradually with the material at hand. Logs. They were flattened a bit and laid side by side. It was called a corduroy road. This provided a bone shaking ride but people started going the short way and have continued to do so as other improvements followed.

We make no apologies for the contents because most of the writing is based on fact. There are only a couple of suppositions. These follow a definite sequence of supportive information. Therefore, in our opinion, to deny the obvious connections would be unjustifiable.

The gathering of settlers to worship was the first assemblage followed shortly by the Gleaner Lodge. Construction of the Chicago and Northeastern Railroad, and building of a fine depot, brought business to the area. A post office was soon located in a general store. Other businesses soon followed.

The size of this community has been generally recognized as a geographical area, not exceeding, three miles in radius as the crow flies.

It is our wish that the material compiled by cooperative effort and presented herein will be retained and cherished by the descendants of those who lived, loved and died in the community of Duffield, Michigan.

Stanley Cozadd Perkins

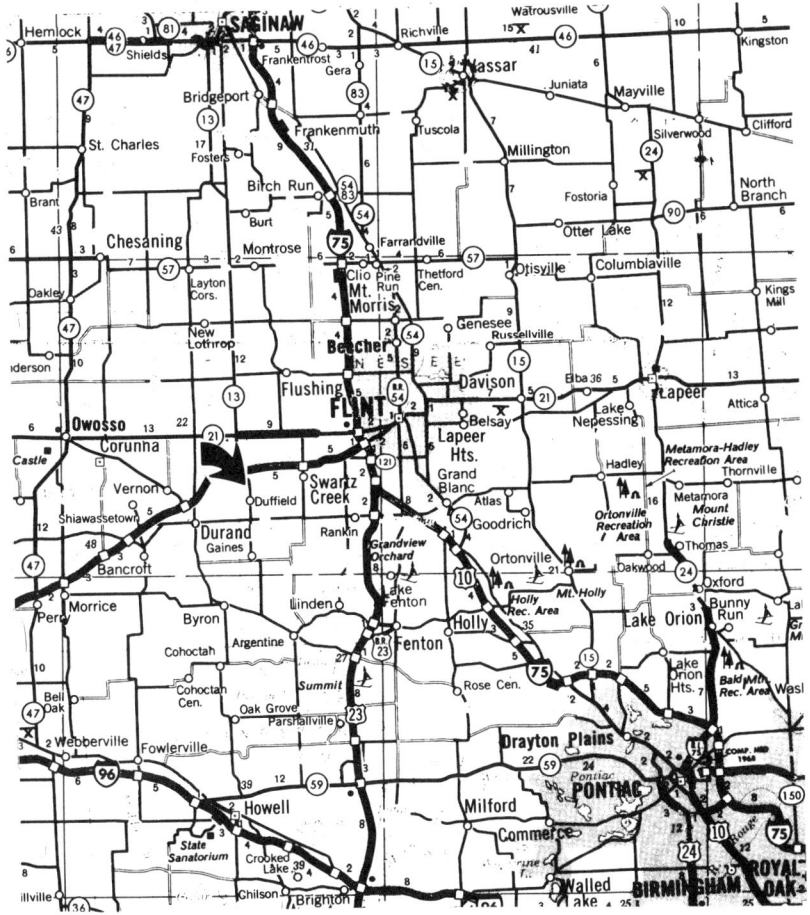

WHERE IS DUFFIELD?

In the southeastern quadrant of Michigan

EDWARD HERRICK FAMILY AND PIONEER HOME

This time exposure was taken in the spring of 1899 at the Herrick steading, at 11333 West Hill Road. It is an example of the well worn statement, "One picture tells a thousand words."

Begin with the display of their trusted driving horse. One can tell he knows this is a special event by the way he has one ear cocked. To the far right, on the front lawn, is the cobblers bench that was used to repair leather goods.

The Edward Herrick family left to right: Robert (Bob), survived by his wife Eva, who lives at 11236 West Reid Road; Erma, daughter who married David Post; Edward, the father was a twin brother of Edwin; Jennie (Rockafellow) Herrick, mother; Verna, daughter who married Curtis Woods and lived directly across the road. And finally, Shep, the family dog was enticed to lay still by giving him his favorite blanket.

The home in the background transcends two eras with the log upright and the clapboard addition.

CHAPTER I

COMMUNITY NAMESAKE

BORN AT CARLISLE, PENNSYLVANIA, December 24, 1833, graduated from University of Michigan 1854 with a B.A., he continued his studies at University of Pennsylvania in 1856. In 1857 he went to Germany for his Ph.D. He studied at Berlin, Hesse, Giessen and Munich in both chemistry and physics. Returning to the United States, thirsting for additional knowledge, this young man claimed his M.D. from Detroit College of Medicine. Shortly thereafter he began a medical practice in Detroit but was never able to shake off his interest in chemistry and the need for better medicine. At some date he journeyed to University of Dorpat in Russia where his theory on toxicology was reinforced: "That the assimilation of minute proportions of recognized poisons could be used as medicine." It flirted with homeopathy.

It is recorded that in the summer and fall of 1871 this already famous self-made man traveled the area of the Shiawassee River watershed and in particular the ridges that provided the headwater areas that separated one watershed from another. He was in search of mineral springs.

There is available a complete analysis of a sample of well water, taken in the vicinity, that he made on September 19th, 1871. His statement on the particular sample went like this, "Belongs to the class of calcareous waters and will be useful in

DR. SAMUEL
PEARCE DUFFIELD

dyspepsia in which there is acidity, also in uric gravel and rheumatism."

He traveled the route of railroad survey parties. One such survey was made by a stock company called the Flint and Lansing Railroad Company, after 1870. It traversed Gaines Township on a northeast diagonal through sections 18, 8 and 9 and crossed property owned at that time by G. Carrier, W. M. Johnson, W. B. Young, F. Whitmore and the Chippewa Fishers. Several springs were on these properties. The search for raw materials to be used for the manufacture of medicines is what brought Dr. Duffield to the area that was in a few years to bear his name.

He and his party, no doubt, quartered with one or more of these families and paid them well for board and lodging. Gifts could have been exchanged. There could have been correspondence and reports of water tests sent back to his friends in Gaines Township. These suppositions are justified because of the natural camaraderie developed and the courtesies exchanged by people of that time.

It has been said, that he was an impressive yet modest man. When the railroad was finally constructed and a depot built in 1876, on a different survey line and by a different stock company, there was no question about what it was to be named. It was called "Duffield Station," for the great man who had made a lasting impression on the landowners of northwestern Gaines Township.

The naming was entirely defendable as subsequent events proved. Dr. Duffield became the founding father of the great Parke Davis & Company in this manner. We quote here from their 100th Anniversary Book.

"European advances in chemistry paved the way for the rudimentary beginnings of the pharmaceutical industry. An early pioneer in this field was Dr. Samuel P. Duffield. While studying chemistry in Germany he conceived the dream of a manufacturing laboratory in his home town. In 1862 he started his business—with serious shortages of capital, equipment and with undependable sources of raw materials."

Several partners entered the business but most withdrew as they realized the size of the challenge. In 1866 Dr. Duffield met Harvey C. Parke, a sound businessman. The partnership of Duffield and Parke was formed. Dr. Duffield handled the technical aspects; Parke, finance and management. Another man was required—a salesman named S. Davis.

Dr. Duffield later sold out his interest before the big bucks arrived. He was Health Officer for Detroit in 1887-98.

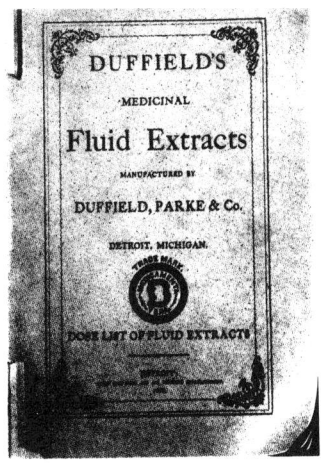

FROM THE
DUFFIELD PARKE
& CO. CATALOG

This catalog was distributed to the professions in 1868.

NEW CHURCH AS CONSTRUCTED IN 1891

Note the buggy tracks in the road and horse sheds behind the church. A dining room was built later below the eaves on the side toward the sheds.

CHAPTER II

THE CHURCH

NOVEMBER 19, 1890 was the recorded date of the organization of the First Methodist Episcopal Church of Duffield, Michigan. The charter members and Board of Trustees were Daniel Brown, Chairman; Dan Proper, Treasurer; G. P. Hardick, Secretary; Jno. Atherton, Thomas Bastian and William Shaw.

For more than 25 years previous to this official action, church services were held in a schoolhouse one mile north on the southeast corner of Hill and Duffield Roads.

Previous to the use of this schoolhouse for worship it is safe to assume that religious gatherings were first held in homes on a rotating basis. During times of stress it was natural for pioneering people to seek consolation and moral support, one from another. It has been recorded that a prayer meeting was held within the community upon receipt of the news of Lincoln's assassination. This would lead us to believe that there was an established group before the War of the Rebellion.

It was an unaffiliated protestant congregation composed of the members of the early families serviced by circuit riding preachers and so-called elders in the community until the year 1871. Then, it seems, a definite schedule of services was formulated so that it was possible for the pastor at Gaines to also serve this charge at the North Duffield School.

Pastors on record before the first church was built were as follows:

T. G. Omens	1871-2	M. E. Lyons	1881-4
D. B. Miller	1872-3	D. J. Odell	1884-5
William Birdsell	1873-5	E. E. Caster	1885-7
E. H. Brockway	1875-7	John Sweet	1887-8
John Wesley	1877-9	Ira Labaron	1889
E. Craven	1879-1		

— SCHEDULE OF SERVICES —
Preaching: 2:30 P.M. — Sunday School 1:30 P.M.
Epworth League: 7:30 P.M. Sunday night
Prayer Meeting: Wednesday evening 7:30 P.M.

Church suppers and large meetings were held in the Gleaner Hall, adjacent to the railroad, on what is now Duffield Road.

A business meeting was called for Monday, November 24, 1890. A motion was made and carried to build a church on the southeast corner of Reid and Duffield Roads. The deed to one half acre of land for this site was given by William M. Johnson from his farm providing that a church be built "within one year from date of deed." "Money in the treasurers hands to date $10.00. The board further decided to meet at this new ground and stake out line for foundation and spend $5.00 for church building plans No. 13T."

On Monday, December 29, the board met at an undesignated location in Duffield and decided to "advertise for sealed proposals received till Feby 1, 1891."

"Feby 9, 1891. Board of trustees met to open proposals for building church. Board decided to reject all bids and advertise by letter changing specifications and using No. 2 shingles and cheaper lumber."

"Feby 27, 1891. Board met to open bids." There was a note that William Shaw was absent and that John Atherton sent in his resignation. No bids were accepted. It appears that there was a difference of opinion at this meeting which was closed by offering one E. Preston $900.00 to build the church.

On March 21, 1891, the board met at the residence of Mr. and Mrs. Dan Proper and finally made a deal with Standard &

The Church

Preston to construct the new church for $1000.00 using "xxx shingles." The terms were $400.00 to be paid upon delivery of materials, $250.00 when the building was enclosed and the balance "within 30 days after dedication."

The building of a church was not without the usual discussions and disagreements. Secretary of the Board, Grant Hardick, resigned at the June 1, 1891 meeting and was replaced by F. S. Mapes. They promptly decided "that the church wall be built 3 ft. above the present level." The cornerstone was laid July 11, with Dan Proper in charge of all the details, followed by a church supper at the Gleaner Hall. The official dedication was still several months hence but the people of the community were enthused about the definite prospects of finally having a church of their own and a tentative program for this ceremony was planned as early as July 2, 1891, when the board instructed their pastor, the Rev. J. F. Emerick, to arrange for speakers and the Gaines Band for music.

— Duffield Dec. 6, 1891 —

Today the Church of Duffield was dedicated. The sermon was preached by Rev. J. E. Jacklin, M.A., of Detroit, Associate Editor of The Michigan Christian Advocate. The text was St. John 3-17. Rev. J. B. Gross of Brent Creek and Rev. W. W. Wall of Swartz Creek were visiting Clergymen.

The Secty F. H. Mapes submitted the following financial report.

Cost of stone-drawing stone-sand-and grading	$ 75.00
Cost of building	1000.00
Foundation	93.00
Furnace	100.00
Seats and painting the same	41.00
Lamps, pulpit, etc.	74.90
Total	$1383.90
Recd on Subscriptions	310.85
Ladies Aid Society	72.80
Donated in work, etc.	90.00
	473.65

Amt. yet to be raised $910.25

The following are the amounts given and subscribed at the dedication:

Board of Church Extensions	$ 150.00
Mrs. Sophia Whitmore	50.00
(referred to elsewhere in records as Aunt Sophie)	
Ladies Aid Society	100.00
Young Peoples Society	50.00
D. C. Proper	50.00
Daniel Brown	50.00
Jno. L. Lee	50.00
F. H. Mapes & wife	50.00
William H. Shaw	25.00
Ezra Fulton	25.00
Mrs. Charles Baxter	20.00
Nelson VanBuskirk	20.00
H. P. Doane	20.00
Jas. Rockafellow & E. Herrick	20.00
Jas. F. Emerick, Pastor	20.00
Mrs. T. N. Bastian	15.00
Mrs. M. Karren	15.00
W. D. Brown	15.00
Wm. A. Merchant	10.00
Mr. & Mrs. George Harle	10.00
Grant Hardick	10.00
Mrs. D. C. Brown	10.00
Jno. Hart	10.00
Fred Beard	10.00
Robt. Passmore	10.00
B. W. Karrer	10.00
Frank Hamlin	10.00
Hugh Gilmore	5.00
Mrs. J. E. Beckwith	5.00
Horace W. Gilbert	5.00
Ed Vincent	5.00
W. S. Waterman	5.00
Seth B. Terry	5.00
S. Hulin	5.00
Francis Whitmore	5.00
C. E. Fox	25.00
Sam C. Goodyear	25.00
Wm. G. Gilmore	10.00
W. H. Watson	10.00
W. H. Sayre	10.00

G. P. Power	10.00
M. A. Simonson	5.00
Mrs. Gilbert-Bennett	5.00
Mrs. J. H. Caster	2.00
Dan McCaughna	1.00
D. Elwood	2.00
Mrs. A. Harris	1.00
Adam Reed	2.00
D. Gilmore	2.00
E. E. Pratt	2.00
M. H. Wolfin	1.00
Wm. Smith	2.00
Wm. Groesbeck	5.00
J. C. Shepherd	3.00
Flora Bennett	1.00
Mrs. G. P. Powen	2.00
Clare Proper	.50
J. & E. Holser	1.00
Ernest Benson	1.00
Wm. Whitmore	1.00
Total	$1004.50
Cost $1383.90	
	- 379.40

Most all of these family names are also recorded on plat maps as farmers or businessmen of the same date.

Not all the goings-on with the congregation of the First Duffield Methodist were serious. They had their happy times even as you and I. True, there were financial problems and heated discussions within the Board of Trustees that were serious enough that some of the trustees literally threw up their hands and walked out. In reference, note the resignations of trustees John Atherton, a storekeeper, and Grant Hardick, a landowner.

At the C. E. Fox home in the early spring of 1892 a surprise party was called for Rev. J. F. Emerick with twenty-six families represented. It could have been a birthday or anniversary with all the proceeds going to the guest. There was visiting, story telling, games, singing around the old organ and finally a shadow social with the most popular man about Duffield town, Uncle Billy Merchant the blacksmith, serving as auctioneer. A shadow social was similar to a box social except the bidder purchased the shadow of a lady by number, as she cavorted back of a white sheet suspended in an archway. A lamp was placed strategically behind her so that an exaggerated image was cast upon the sheet. The bidders (men) sat in an adjoining darkened room. A total of $47.00 was raised. It is recorded that D. Brown paid the top price of $7.50 for something that appealed to him. Other top prices were paid by D. C. Proper, $5.25 and T. N. Bastian at $3.50. Wm. Merchant, the auctioneer, picked off a shadow for only $1.25, but there is a listing near the end that tells something about the weakness of this village smithy. "Wm. Merchant for cake 10¢."

Along in January of 1896 there was a blow up about something. Francis Whitmore, Jas. Goodrich, John L. Lee and F. H. Mapes were the board members present when this line was a portion of the minutes: "that the Secretary—notify Mr. Proper that they have not given him the authority to sue the note he holds agains Mr. C. E. Fox and that they will not stand by him in the suit."

Another board meeting was held the next week "Jany, 20th, 96." Within the brief minutes is this statement; "Moved and supported that Mr. Mapes goes down to Flint and pays the cost and withdraws the suit of Mr. Fox's—carried." A postscript follows: "Duffield Mich. Jany. 21, 1896. This day I, F. H. Mapes have been to Flint and withdrawn the suit of his; C. E. Fox and paid the cost the total of which was all told $3.75."

This was serious trouble of some sort between Proper and Fox. It was a civil suit over payment of a note and it is doubtful if it had anything to do with the church. It appears that the church board moved in to take the role of peacemaker betweeen two of its members.

The writer appreciates the interest that readers might have in attempting to unravel this mystery. Stress was visible in the quality of the penmanship as written by the Secretary, Frank H. Mapes.

Following these struggling years of building and paying for the church with deflated currency, there is a span of time for which no records are available except what can be lifted from reports of the Ladies Aid Society.

The Church

All official records of the Duffield Methodist Church were lost on June 8th, 1953, when a death dealing tornado hit a district to the north of Flint. Genevra Stottlemeyer and Jean Addison, ministers at that date, resided in the devastated area. Both were injured in this storm. All their worldly goods were destroyed along with the membership lists and minutes of all the meetings held in the Duffield Church from 1896 to 1953. This was a severe historical loss, by an act of God, but no reason is available on why these valuable records were removed from church property.

A reconstructed account of happenings and activities of devoted people, from related and sometimes vague sources, follows for this fifty-nine year period.

In addition to those previously mentioned as trustees on the early boards, we are listing here, alphabetically, men of the Duffield Church who were active before the period of the lost records and to the present date of publication:

Ackerman, Floyd
Ackerman, Frank II
Ackerman, Frederick
Ackerman, William, Jr.
Ackerman, William, Sr.
Allen, Frank
Atherton, W. R.
Atkinson, William
Beard, Harry
Beckwith, D.
Beckwith, William
Bennett, Kenneth
Boist, Walter R.
Boist, Wray S.
Brown, Daniel
Brown, Ernest I.
Brown, Hiram
Brown, Ira
Brown, S. H.
Brown, W. K.
Buchanan, Lyle
Burns, John J.
Burton, Charles

Burton, Dwight
Burton, Hamp
Burton, John
Burton, Putnam
Carrier, Adelbert W.
Carrier, Delbert L.
Carrier, Arthur G.
Carrier, George L.
Carrier, Lyman E.
Chapman, Edward
Clark, Jerome
Coffield, Floyd
Cohoon, Arthur
Crane, Albert
Cranner, Alfonso
Davenport, Arthur
Deake, Augustus
Deake, Ellsworth
Drlik, John
Drlik, Paul
Drummond, Milton
DuPraw, Vernon
Edwards, Donald

Edwards, Lawrence
Ferguson, A. J.
Ferguson, James
Fox, Eugene
Gensel, Wm. Dr.
Gilbert, Wayne
Gilmore, Edward H.
Gilmore, Marshal
Gilmore, Ward
Gilmore, William
Goodrich, James
Goodrich, Harry
Gunsell, Garry
Hale, Richard
Hale, Sanford
Hale, William
Hamlin, Clarence
Hardick, LeGrant
Harle, Glen
Harle, George J.
Harris, Leroy
Harris, George
Harris, William R.

Harding, Frank
Harnick, Brad
Hasyn, David
Herrick, Edward
Herrick, Edwin
Herrick, Robert
Hillaker, Benjamin
Jennings, J. P.
Johnson, Harley
Jones, Daniel
Jones, John R.
Judson, Ephriam
Judson, Russell
Kerr, Frank
Kimble, Martin
Lee, Jno. L.
Lewis, James
Mapes, Frank H.
McCartney, Roy
McDonald, James
McLaren, Lloyd
McLaren, Michael
McLaren, Norman
Merchant, Wm.
Middlesworth, John J.
Myers, F.
Nemecek, John
Nimphie, George
Nimphie, Henry G.

Nimphie, John
Nimphie, Roy
Parker, Ardon
Parker, Robert
Parks, Charles
Partridge, Darwin
Passmore, Lewis
Passmore, Robert
Perkins, Elmer
Perkins, Fenton
Perkins, George
Perkins, Lyman
Perkins, Preston
Perkins, Stan C.
Perkins, Wm. S.
Porter, Charles
Porter, George
Post, Carl
Post, Edgar
Post, David
Post, Harold L.
Post, John
Post, John II
Proper, Clare
Purdy, Henry
Purdy, Lee
Purdy, Neal
Purdy, Phillip
Purdy, Wayne

Raver, Wayne Dr.
Redman, Everett
Robertson, Gordon F.
Sharp, Robert L.
Shaw, William
Smedley, Elky
Stacer, Carl
Stender, Wesley J.
Swan, Ernest
Teeters, Noble
Teller, William
Terry, Elisha
Terry, Isaac
Terry, Seth
Thomas, George
Van Buskirk, N.
Van Tifflin, Wm.
Vincent, Edward
Warren, James
Warren, John
Weller, Russell
Wheeler, Howard H.
Wheeler, Howard J.
Whitmore, Frank
Woods, Clyde
Woods, Curtis
Woods, Harry
Woods, Richard

Pastors during the building of the church and to this current publishing are listed herewith:

J. F. Emerick	1889-93	Leonard Hazard	1910-11
J. B. Goss	1893-94	Franklin Bradley	1911-13
Robert Emerick	1894-95	Otto J. Lyon	1913-15
Joseph Ryerson	1895-98	M. H. Bartran	1915-16
S. W. Bird	1898-02	M. R. Reed	1916-17
R. Patterson	1902-03	J. A. Garman	1917-18
D. C. Challis	1903-05	J. B. Wallace	1918-21
George W. Wright	1905-08	E. L. Carless	1921-23
C. W. Scott	1908-10	W. P. Ainsworth	1923-25

The Church

J. J. Strike	1925-26	H. L. Kemp	1959-61
Arthur C. Tinglan	1926-34	C. D. Arrand	1961-63
J. Harris Williams	1934-39	Ellis L. Fenton	1963-67
Horace L. James	1939-40	Gordon F. Robertson	1967-68
Frank Miner	1940-41	Donald E. Hall	1968-69
Leonard Kemp	1941-45	Donald D. McLellan	1969-70
Dwight A. Lawson	1945-46	Gary L. Sanderson	1970-71
Leonard Kemp	1946-48	Herbert W. Thompson	1971-77
William J. Blight	1948-49	Bruce W. Garner	1977-79
Genevra Stottlemeyer	1949-53	Paul I. Greer	1979-81
Jean A. Addison	1953-54	Thomas E. Adams, Jr.	1981-82
Donald Devey	1954-56	Meredith Moshauer	1982-
Wayne W. Brookshear	1956-59		

There could be the names of numerous supply pastors added to this list.

SAMUEL W. BIRD, PASTOR, 1898-1902

THE DUFFIELD CHURCH, 1899

CHAPTER III

THE DUFFIELD LADIES AID SOCIETY

(Woman's Society of Christian Service)
(1969 United Methodist Women)

THE ORGANIZATIONAL MEETING was held March 3, 1891 at Dan Brown's home. The charter members and officers elected for six months were: Mrs. S. E. Brown, President; Mrs. Sophie Whitmore, Vice President; Mrs. D. C. Proper, Secretary; Mrs. William Shaw, Treasurer; Jennie Herrick, Verna Burton, Lucie Lee, Sara Fox, Mrs. E. G. Vincent, Mrs. C. M. Hardick, Mrs. A. F. Fulton, Mrs. C. R. Bastian, Mrs. F. Myers, Mrs. William Merchant, Allie Proper, Carrie Brown and Mrs. H. Harris.

By-laws were adopted consisting of nine articles. Seven of these by-laws were routine. Two were not. They had to do with the food that the hostess would serve as the society made a circuit of the various homes in the parish and the fare that would be served at church suppers. By reading between the lines it is evident that this was a touchy subject and that much discussion had taken place. Could this have been some sort of limitation placed on the quantity of food in the various dinners so that one hostess would not upstage another with a more impressive event? It appears to have been a set of restrictions to keep the society on an even keel.

Dues were established at 10¢ per month with a provision for visitors to pay a like amount for their dinner. Visitors totaled 96 for the first year with receipts of $9.80. Someone paid double.

The first order drawn on the treasurer was for $5.40 on July 2, 1891. It further states that "it was lain by."

At the same meeting "arrangements were made for getting a supper when the cornerstone of the new church is put in place by a committee being chosen to go around and see what we could get donated in the eating line." The money received from the cornerstone laying supper was $20.37 plus $5.23 for ice cream dessert and $20.16 from a quilt raffle.

This Ladies Society has been the right arm of the church since the beginning. At their December 6th, 1891 meeting they pledged $100.00 to be paid "in two years" toward the cost of the new church building. During 1892 the following new members were secured: Mrs. Lucretia Hale, Mrs. Lena Perkins, Mrs. F. D. Blake, Mrs. Della VanTifflin, Mrs. John Ryno, Mrs. J. P. Jennings, Minnie Carrier, Ida Shaw, Mrs. A. Marshall, Jennie Countryman, Mrs. M. W. Carrier, Mrs. Jerome Clark, Mrs. Myra Myres, Mrs. Nettie Perkins, Mrs. Eva Burton, Mrs. Jane Beckwith and Mrs. Sarah Hamlin. Mrs. H. Harris' name was crossed off and Allie Proper had changed her name to Passmore. Some young man plucked himself a rose.

The reports of this Ladies Society go on for years and years, telling the story of devotion to their church and community. We have lifted the minutes of a typical meeting and reprint it here verbatim.

January 11, 1894

> The Ladies met at Mrs. Carriers, a cold day, but a very good attendance. The meeting was opened by reading and prayer by the President. Pieces were read by Mrs. Ira Brown and Mrs. Nettie Perkins. A motion was made and supported—the Ladies hold a Church Fair. Carried. Motion made and supported—the Ladies make a worsted quilt to be sold for the benefit of the society.

The Duffield Ladies Aid Society

The President appointed Mrs. VanTiflin, Mrs. Proper and Mrs. Bastian to contribute literary entertainment at the next meeting at Mrs. Preston Perkins'.

No. of members present	17
No. of Visitors	12
Amt. received	$3.13

It could be of interest to the reader that the minutes above were copied from a leftover Civil War Ledger of The Woman's Relief Corps No. 19 Grand Army of the Republic, printed by E. B. Stillings, Boston, Mass.

Following are additional parcels and bits of information selected from various reports of the Duffield Ladies Aid Society thought to be of interest.

Millie Chapman's Treasurers report for the year 1918-19 was in this groove. Here are some excerpts.

Sept. 15	Receipts at Mrs. Whitmores	$ 6.45
Oct. 3	Receipts at Mrs. Perkins	11.95
Nov.	No Aid on account of Influenza	
Dec.	No Aid on account of Influenza	
Jan. 30	Receipts at Mrs. Deakes	13.15
Feb. 8	Fish Dinner	29.00
Mar. 7	Young Peoples dinner at Gleaner Hall	9.65
Apr. 10	Receipts at Mrs. Chapmans	7.00
May 1	Receipts at Mrs. Allens	14.25
June 5	Receipts at Mrs. Parkers	17.10
July 17	Receipts at Mrs. Nimphies	15.60
Aug. 7	Annual Picnic, Myers Lake	21.12

Some of the Expenses

Jan. 30	Wm. Merchant, janitor work	11.90
Jan. 30	Mrs. Middlesworth, coal and flowers	18.03
Mar. 8	Walter Boist, piano tuning	.75

In this report there were four other entries for funeral flowers. These were because of the flu epidemic that swept the country during the severe winter of 1918. On November 11, 1918,

Armistice was declared. The whole countryside was down in bed with the flu. Remembered well are the church bells and train whistles. There was little celebrating in Duffield because most everyone was flat in bed with a high fever and extreme congestion.

January 8, 1925 taken from the D.L.A. minutes.

> President Lillian Deake appointed Mr. & Mrs. Edward Gilmore and Mr. & Mrs. William Harris to work with the Gleaner committee in getting the Gleaner Hall ready to be used as a community house.
>
> Secretary Elma Ackerman

> April 11, 1925
> "Served dinner at John Posts cattle auction. There were over 300 served. There was cleared $47.20."
>
> Sec. E. Ackerman

> May 2, 1925
> "Motion was made and supported to have Ed Gilmore put a lock on the church door."
>
> Sec. E. Ackerman

> November 1, 1928
> "New dining hall used by D.L.A. first time."
>
> Sec. Mrs. E. J. McMichael

Comment here could be that the men were an integral part of this D.L.A. except they had no jurisdiction over the cash box. There are many entries in the treasurer's report where they paid the minister's salary. They paid for the wood and coal. They bought shingles for the roof, etc. The Ladies Society did the paying. Individual men did the labor. United we stand. Divided we did the work.

Here is a reminiscing set of minutes that you might like to read. It is taken from the November 1931 minutes, a short time before the much remembered Bank Holiday.

> The Ladies Aid Society met at the Hall. An Old Fashioned Boiled Dinner was served at noon. The time was used working

on quilts. Meeting was called to order by President Blanche Haist. Motion was made and supported to charge 35¢ for our chicken dinner. The motion was lost. A motion was then made and supported to charge adults 50¢ and children under fifteen 25¢. Motion carried. It was decided to loan the Aid Society of Lennon 50 table services. Floral collection 22¢. Dues and dinner collection $4.90.

Myrtle Baird, Secy.

Here is a program from the May 25, 1934 Mother and Daughter Banquet held in the dining room on the south side of the church.

    Doxology — Mother and Daughters
    Greetings — Bernice Brown
    Invocation — Mrs. Claxton
    Banquet Dinner
    Introduction of Toastmistress by Margaret Gilmore
    Vocal Duet — Atheline Claxton & June McMichael
    Violin Solo — Miss Geraldine Wade
    Toast to Mothers — Miss Marian Post
    Toast to Daughters — Mrs. Myrtle Baird
    Vocal Duet — Mrs. Sayre & Mrs. Deake
    Address — Mrs. Romily H. Prouse, Swartz Creek
      (wife of Swartz Creek pastor)
    Benediction — Proceeds $10.18

Riddle—Who was the Toastmistress?

When the fine women of the D.L.A. were sometimes secluded by themselves, as at a Mother and Daughter Banquet the likes of the one above, they were apt to loosen their corset lacings a bit and let go with lusty and sometimes boisterous songfests. In other words, they would relax from the drudgery of the daily tasks as their menfolk would do while at the Owls Nest.

For these songfests song books were a must. One of these books has survived. It was found betwixt the back pages of an ancient Secretary-Treasurers ledger. Reluctantly it came forth to the light of day fragile and yellowed. On page twenty there is a ditty to be sung to the tune of Auld Lang Syne. It was simply titled.

MULES

On mules we find two legs behind,
And two we find before,
We stand behind, before we find
What the two behind are for;
When we're behind the two behind,
We find what these be for.
So stand before the two behind
And behind the two before.

There will be no futher comment upon the subject and no more exposure of its contents. It has been returned from thence it came, perhaps forever.

One of the things that the Duffield Ladies have always done best, is cook. Their church suppers are the best in the land. They have never been selfish about sharing their culinary secrets with others. Each generation has pooled its talents and published a book of favorite recipes, together with advertising by local merchants, as a money raising project.

On the back page of "The Home Cook Book," a book of kitchen tested recipes prepared and published by the Ladies of the Methodist Church, Duffield, Michigan in 1940, is the following information for:

CLUB OR CHURCH SUPPERS

Fish — one fourth pound per person
Meat — one fourth pound per person
Fowl — one third pound per person
Butter — one pound for 25 servings
Bread — one loaf for 14 or 15 people
Potatoes — one Bushel, uncooked for 100 servings
Ice Cream — one gallon for 32 servings
Coffee — one pound for 30 cups
Tea — one pound for 50 cups
Cake — one cake for 12 to 16 servings
Pie — six servings to each pie
Sandwiches — two and one half pounds butter will spread 100 sandwiches.

A cook book was also published in 1955 and another one is past due.

The Duffield Ladies Aid Society

At the present time the United Methodist Women is still the most active branch of the church. To support the fact here is a synopsis report for the fall of 1981.

President — Ardis (Brown) McLaren
Vice President — Marjorie (Hill) Woods
Secretary — Iva (Johnson) McMichael
Treasurer — Catherine (Drlik) Nemecek
Flower Fund — Mona (Rinker) Gilbert

Financial statement on turkey supper October 29, 1981	
Gross @ $4.00 for adults $2.50 for juniors	$663.95
Expenses for supper	83.50
Net	$580.45
Sales from Bazaar held at same time	165.75
Total receipts from event	$746.20

Kitchen Chairman — Naoma (Frasier) Perkins
Dining room Chairman — Ardis (Brown) McLaren

Their monthly meetings are usually held in private homes. Refreshments are served. Dues are 50¢ per month.

Projects completed with new materials were:
Pieced and sold quilt.
Dossal drapes for sanctuary.
Carpet runner for main aisle.
Folding doors for back stairway.

They are very appreciative of the two new stoves and new refrigerator presented by the Beards family in memory of their mother, Bessie, and the gift of a stove by Helen (Drlik) Kadlechick.

As the years have spun away there has been a normal attrition within the society. Being a member usually signified that the family was active in the Duffield Church. We are indebted to some old records, volunteers and just nice people for assisting us in compiling this incomplete list. Your mother, grandmother, great-grandmother or great-great-grandmother's name could be included in this list of participants if she lived within a buggy ride distance of Duffield.

Ackerman, Elma
Ackerman, Evlyn
Ackerman, Marguerite
Ackerman, Sarah
Ackerman, Shirley
Allen, Flora
Atherton, Anna
Atherton, Myrtle
Atkinson, Esther
Atkinson, Opal
Baird, Myrtle
Barker, Marie
Beard, Bessie
Beckwith, Mrs. D.
Beckwith, Lizzie
Bellis, Maude
Bemis, Grace
Bemis, Hazel
Bloss, Eunice
Boist, Dora
Boring, Mrs.
Bradley, Mrs.
Brown, Bernice
Brown, Carrie A.
Brown, Ella
Brown, Sarah
Brown, Vera
Buchanan, Delloise
Buchanan, Nancy
Burton, Eva
Burton, Ruth
Burton, Verna
Bush, Edith
Bush, Lila
Bush, Maxine
Byam, Elizabeth
Carrier, Maria
Carrier, Mary
Chapman, Bernice
Chapman, Millie
Chase, Dora
Christie, Mary L.
Clark, Delia
Claxton, Sylvia

Coffield, Barbara
Cohoon, Phyllis
Coryelle, Maxine
Cox, Mary E.
Crane, Mrs. Albert
Crippen, Ida
Danner, Anna
Dart, Gladys
Davenport, Mrs. A.
Deake, Mrs. Augustus
Deake, Lillian
Drlik, Anna
Drlik, Beth
Drlik, Eva
Drlik, Helen
Drlik, Vera
Dyal, Ethel
Eckel, Audrey
Edison, Mrs.
Edwards, Grace
Edwards, Viva
Ferguson, Althea
Ferguson, Anna
Fowler, Belle
Fox, Mrs. Eugene
Fredericks, Cora
Fredericks, Mildred
Fulton, Mrs. E.
Fulton, Josie
Gensel, Mary
Gensel, Nellie
Gilbert, Marguerite
Gilbert, Mona
Gilmore, Alta
Gilmore, Florence
Gilmore, Mary
Gilmore, Minda
Goodman, Ann
Goodman, Elizabeth
Goodrich, Mrs. James
Hackney, Donna
Haist, Blanche
Hale, Esther
Hale, Mildred

Hamper, Belle
Hardick, Mrs. Grant
Hardin, Ruth
Harding, Frances
Harding, Nellie
Harle, Della
Harris, Helen
Harris, Mrs. H.
Harris, Nell
Holmes, Betty
Hudson, Ada
Jenkins, Florence
Jennings, Agnes
Jennings, Olive
Johnson, Belle
Jones, Mrs. John R.
Judson, Beulah
Kanaar, June
Keeran, Ruth
Kerr, Elsie
Kimble, Mildred M.
Lahring, Jessie
Lee, Mrs. John L.
Lewis, Phyllis
Lovegrove, Loretta
Luce, Maggie
Lyon, Bertha
Mapes, Josephine
Marshall, Rose
Martin, Margaret
Martin, Pearl
McCaughna, Jennette
McDonald, Mrs. James
McLaren, Ardis
McLaren, Cathryn
McLaren, Janet
McLaren, Melissa
McMichael, Mattie
McMichael, June
McMichael, Iva
McMichael, Maude
Merchant, Libbie
Middlesworth, Mable
Morgan, Florence

The Duffield Ladies Aid Society

Morgan, Joyce
Morgan, Louise
Morgan, Martha
Morgan, Muriel
Mosholder, Shirley
Nemecek, Catherine
Nimphie, Clara
Nimphie, Ella
Nimphie, Hazel
Nimphie, Rose
Ormiston, Maude
Oesterle, Bertha
Oesterle, Inez
Oesterle, Marjorie
Parker, Mrs. Ardon
Parker, Ardonna
Parker, Lillie
Parker, Marjorie
Parks, Sharley Rose
Passmore, Mrs. Robert
Pavlik, Lillian
Perkins, Dorothy
Perkins, Lena
Perkins, Mable
Perkins, Naoma
Perkins, Nettie
Perkins, Rubena B.

Perkins, Sayde
Porter, Jennie
Post, Beverly
Post, Bula
Post, Ermie
Post, Geraldine
Post, Hattie
Post, Marian
Post, Theo
Purdy, Beth
Raver, Onva
Redmond, Clarissa
Robertson, Joyce
Robertson, Mildred
Ruby, Thresa
Ryno, Emma
Ryno, Mary
Sage, Mrs. Wm.
Sayre, Mrs. Fred
Scott, Mrs.
Sharp, Sharon
Shaw, Martha
Slawson, Mable
Smedley, Nellie
Smith, Lucy
Stender, Evelyn
Swan, Mable

Swan, Olive
Syring, Beatrice
Teeter, Jean
Teller, Mrs. N.
Terry, Mrs. Seth
Thomas, Ena
Thomas, Maude
Vanbuskirk, Mrs. E.
Vanbuskirk, Mrs. Wm.
Vincent, Mrs. Elmer
Warren, Mrs. James
Warren, Thelma
Weller, Rose
Wheeler, Dorothy
Wheeler, Rhea
Whitmore, Mrs. Frank
Whitney, Minnie
Woods, Bertha
Woods, Bessie
Woods, Florence
Woods, Helen
Woods, Marjorie
Woods, Verna
Woodthorpe, Pearl
Wykes, Agatha
Yelinek, Emma
Yerkes, Addie

THE CHURCH AS REBUILT

CHAPTER IV

THE FIRE

THE ROUTINE was interrupted on Sunday, January 22, 1939 when this treasured edifice was consumed by fire. An otherwise devoted townsman built up a fire in the furnace, which was in the southwest corner of the sanctuary. He returned to his store on the catercorner, leaving the draft open. The fire became the master instead of the servant before he returned. The pews, vestments and some records were saved and are being used yet today.

Condolences were rendered. Offers were tendered by churches of all denominations in adjacent towns for the free use of their facilities. One letter, in particular, should be mentioned here. It was a gracious handwritten note signed by Zoah Miller, secretary of the Swartz Creek Community Methodist Church, at the bidding of her official board, in which this competitor for local parishioners offered the use of their church to the Duffield congregation.

As independent proud country people they brushed all offers aside and returned to holding services in the North Duffield School, a site they had last used for worship 47 years plus 2 months previous.

The men of the community were determined, resourceful and talented. In addition they were agreeable one to another and used to working cooperatively in their daily tasks. This was a paradoxical atmosphere far removed from the situation that existed when the first church was constructed. It was looked upon as a barn raising would be for your next door neighbor. In this instance the church was everyone's next door neighbor.

The men, and the women for their supportive efforts, are to be commended as unsung heroes, for the giving of their labor and talents. Actions of this type, by public spirited unselfish people, are what have made this the great nation that it is. This bootstrap project could be plucked from actuality to serve as a prime example of Americana. This is one of the credits that can be bestowed not only upon this typical community in Gaines Township of Genesee County, Michigan, but throughout the width and breadth of this land. It is a fine demonstration of the resourcefulness of its people.

These men of the Duffield Methodist Church, and the entire community that included some very stable Irish Catholic families, went to work. A building committee consisting of Richard Hale, Ernest Swan, Edward McMichael, Floyd Ackerman and Ernest Brown accepted the challenge. Ample support was provided by:

Harry Woods	William Ackerman	Ben Hillaker
John Post	Burdette McMichael	Frank Hynes
David Post	Paul Drlik	William Hynes
William Harris	Charles Brugger	Martin Drlik
Frank Ackerman	Willsey Rice	Ed Gilmore
Roy Nimphie	Ellsworth Deake	Robert Herrick
John Drlik	Emil Drlik	

Ernest Brown was the top honcho on the masonry. Volunteer common labor was not difficult to come by. The women kept ample foodstuffs available and were always willing to run errands.

Selected logs were donated by Paul Drlik, Richard Hale, Crapo Farms, Ernest Parker, Roy Nimphie, Ernest Swan, Martin Vodden, Dr. Wm. Gensel, James Aurand, John Post & Sons, Ellsworth Deake, Curtis Woods, Ben Hillaker and William Harris.

The sawing was done by John Post on Frank Ackerman's mill with the Reeves 20HP steam threshing engine for power. Sometimes the saw would get dull and would put into some of the rafters, studs, and joists what they called a "rainbow twist." This would irk the head carpenter, but since Floyd Ackerman and John Post had each picked themselves off a beautiful daughter of John J. Middlesworth's for a spouse, Evlyn and Bula, respectively, nothing ever came of these minor differences.

Enough of this romancing. Let us get on with the rebuilding of the church. The result is the present structure with alterations.

The basement excavating was begun soon after summer harvest in 1939. Three teams of horses, a walking plow and scoop scrapers were used. Harry Woods' team was named Ned and Babe. Ernest Swan's horses were Topsy and Gyp. Burdette McMichael drove a pair of black Belgians, Jack and Don. An incline was left at each end of the excavation so that the teams

BULA AND EVLYN MIDDLESWORTH

The three Middlesworth girls were the pride of Duffield. Bula, who became Mrs. John Post, and Evlyn, who became Mrs. Floyd Ackerman, are pictured as teenagers.

MERLE MIDDLESWORTH AND WILLIAM KEERAN

Merle is pictured with husband-to-be William Keeran on the depot platform in Duffield waiting for the passenger train to take them to Flint for an evening of entertainment.

This picture was taken at the first depot that was located on the north side of the tracks on space that is now Mrs. Florence Jenkins' flower garden.

could go down one incline and up the other with their loads of dirt. Footings and final squaring were all pick and shovel work. The dimensions were 26 by 40 feet. Footings, floor, and cement stairways were poured with Ernie Brown as overseer. A man from Linden laid the blocks. This basement provided space for the heating plant, kitchen, dining room and the rest rooms. It doubled the floor space.

An I beam was purchased from the Flint Structural Steel Company, almost forty foot long for $16.50, to lay floor joists on and thus support the floor of the sanctuary. Nails were bought for four cents a pound. Cement was purchased at the Gaines Lumber Company for $2.25 a barrel as well as pine lumber at $80.00 per thousand board feet. Ellsworth Deake was in advanced years and physically unable to be a pick and shovel man so he paid Sturtevant & Blood Co. of Owosso $24.93 for

THE FIRE 29

ripping and dressing 56 pieces of 4×6's and 1308' of 4" boards as his contribution. It was picked up August 31, 1939. Dallas E. Hibbard, of out Byron way, charged only $53.41 for all electrical work including materials. The furnace was purchased from a good Irishman, F. J. Mahoney, of Owosso, for $140.00, and so that is the way it was.

All of these financial quotes are from actual bills. They were all purchased at wholesale or less. In addition, there were many other unsung heroes that we who are using this facility today are forever indebted.

And here is the rest of the story. When completed, the building debt was only $367.19. Insurance received was $1900.00. And so—the great little church arose from the ashes of the past. It could be said that it was reborn—or born again. Take your choice.

The dedication of this replacement Duffield Methodist Church took place on Sunday, April 27, 1941.

Pastors present were:

    Rev. E. L. Carless, Lennon
    Rev. Frank Minor, Kearsley Church, Flint
    Rev. Otto J. Lyon, Novi
    Rev. Arthur E. Tinglan, Owosso
    Rev. Leonard Kemp, Flint

The Kearsley Street Methodist Church Choir accompanied Rev. Minor from Flint and assisted in making the dedication first class. At the afternoon service 123 were present. It was a homecoming type worship. Some of the former members and friends that attended with other addresses were:

    Mr. and Mrs. Ernest Kurtz, Williamston
    Mr. and Mrs. Ora Sessions, Monroe
    Mr. and Mrs. Wm. Wooley, Lennon
    Mr. and Mrs. Ulysses Dieck, Lennon
    Mr. and Mrs. Henry Newton, Swartz Creek
    Mrs. Rose Nimphie, Swartz Creek
    Mable (Harle) Perkins, Flint
    Glen Harle, Flint
    Verna Burton, Detroit

Laura Shaw, Swartz Creek
Mrs. D. McCaughna, Durand
Mrs. Anna Ferguson, Durand
Mrs. John Coquigne, Rankin
Mrs. Wilbur Short, Swartz Creek
Mrs. Colbrath, Gaines
Mrs. Ruth Burton, Swartz Creek
Mr. and Mrs. Ward Gilmore, Gaines
Mr. and Mrs. Charles Porter, Swartz Creek
Mr. and Mrs. Fred West, Durand
Mr. and Mrs. John Shepherd, Gaines

Collections for the Dedication were $252.55

Secretary, Bula Post

This renewed church with its stable congregation returned to the routine of social events and worship services. However, a new generation blossomed forth at this time and there was great activity in the Sunday School, the Epworth League and a bit later in the Methodist Youth Fellowship as emphasized in the section on youth.

A news story of the event follows:

Duffield Methodist Church
Celebrates 10th Anniversary
Since Rebuilding After Big Fire

Around 85 people attended the anniversary service held at Duffield Methodist Church Sunday, in celebration of the tenth anniversary of the re-building of the church. The original church was destroyed by fire.

Among the visitors were the Rev. Frank Miner, who was pastor of the church when it was dedicated in 1941, who gave the invocation; the Rev. Tinglan, who served the church 16 years ago and is now at Lum, gave the scripture reading.

DR. KLONTZ, district superintendent, gave the morning message, speaking on the "Survival of the Church." The Rev. Kemp, minister when the old church burned, also spoke and the Rev. W. J. Blight, who served the church as pastor in 1949, gave the benediction. The history of the church was given by Mrs. John Post Sr.

Following the anniversary service lunch was served in the church parlors.

The Fire

On October 29, 1957 Wayne and Beth Purdy gave a piece of land 40' by the width of the church lot which is 185'4" as an extension behind the church for additional parking space. This is to revert back to the farm if its use is discontinued for church purposes.

Spruce trees were planted on the church property in Sept. 1964 by Lyle Buchanan.

A major exterior overhaul was done during October of 1974 when white aluminum siding was applied over the somewhat drab and weary insul-brick. The donations from people of the area totaled $2203.12 with the labor furnished once again by the men of the community. Since the passing of Floyd Ackerman, Wayne Gilbert has become foreman and the main push on improvement projects.

Six full length stained glass windows were installed in the church during 1980-81.

In memory of:

Neal D. Purdy
By the Purdy Family

Bernice and Ernest Brown
By their children Ardis, Donna and Robert

Mr. and Mrs. William S. Perkins
By Stan and Naoma Perkins

Mr. and Mrs. William Harris and Eleanor
By the Willard and James Harris Families

John E. and Bula Post
John D. and Edgar Post
By the Post Families

The Carrier Family
By Lyle and Delloise Buchanan

Identification is by way of inscribed brass plaques attached to the bottom of each window frame.

MR. AND MRS. JOHN BURNS ADMIRE WINDOW

Mr. and Mrs. John Burns admiring one of the six stained glass windows as crafted by Henry Purdy.

Henry Purdy, with assistance of his wife, Marjolaine, designed, cut, leaded and installed these valuable additions to the sanctuary.

Funds were given by the Drlik Family in memory of Paul Drlik who passed away in Florida on Thanksgiving Day 1981, to build a steeple on the church. After consultation it was decided to include a belfry, as well. Two bells were made available and the one from the estate of Edward Woods, great-grandfather of Richard Woods, was chosen for the honor of tolling out the various services. It was donated by Lyle and Delloise (Carrier) Buchanan. She, likewise, was the fourth generation removed from Ed Woods, whose home still remains at 10435 Miller Road.

Wayne Gilbert and Albert Nelson constructed the unit in Nelson's shop so precisely that it went into place without alterations. Assisting with the precarious installation on Wednesday, April 7, 1982 were James Bailey, John Burns, Dr. Wayne Raver and Wayne Purdy.

Betty Brenner, Religion Editor of the Flint Journal, composed a fine lead article complete with a photo on this subject that was published April 9, 1982. The headline read "A Gifted Church Member's Talent Becomes Apparent."

Duffield First Methodist Episcopal Church was changed to Duffield United Methodist Church at the Conference in 1969 when a union was officially consummated with the United Brethern Churches.

At least two young men have gone into the ministry from the Duffield Methodist Church. They are recorded on February 8, 1966 as Carl Stacer and Ronald Huff. There may have been others.

In addition there have been many Elders and Lay Leaders that have approached this status in an unofficial manner. Compiling a list from the dim past to the present could include, among others:

Lyle Martin	Aunt Sophie Whitmore
Florence Morgan	Augustus Deake
John Warren, Sr.	Dan Proper
Daniel Brown	Marguerite Ackerman
Ed Gilmore	John Burns

Often these people are more influential in molding a community by their voluntary everyday living and efforts than a steady parade of pastors whose teachings do not necessarily coincide with his predecessor or the one that follows. Also, they

UP GOES THE SPIRE

Top to bottom: Jim Bailey, Wayne Gilbert and Albert Nelson hoisting the spire to adorn the new belfry.

are not obligated to anyone or is it imperative that they compromise their point of view to retain their position. People of this quality are to be revered.

DUFFIELD UNITED METHODIST CHURCH OFFICERS FOR 1982

Lay Member to Annual Conference	Lyle Martin
Church Lay Leader	Florence Morgan
Chairperson, Committee on Finance	Marian Newman
Recording Secretary	Marjorie Woods
Career Planning & Counseling	Iva McMichael
Church Treasurer	Wayne Purdy
Communion Steward	Marjorie Woods
Historian	Delloise Buchanan

WORK AREA CHAIRPERSONS:

Ecumenical Affairs	Pearl Martin
Education	Dorothy Wheeler
Missions	Iva McMichael
Social Concerns, Religion & Race	Stan Perkins
Worship	Marguerite Ackerman

AGE LEVEL CO-ORDINATORS:

Children	Dorothy Wheeler
Youth	Beverly Post
Adult Ministries	Florence Morgan
Family Ministries	Marguerite Ackerman
Musical Director	Janet L. McLaren

BOARD OF TRUSTEES

1982	1983	1984
Lyle Buchanan	Wayne Gilbert	John Drlik
Marjorie Woods	Lyle Martin	Stan Perkins
Ardis McLaren	Dorothy Wheeler	Wayne Purdy

PASTOR-PARISH RELATIONS COMMITTEE

1982	1983	1984
Dorothy Wheeler	Stan Perkins	Beth Purdy
Marian Newman	Naoma Perkins	Lyle Martin

COMMITTEE ON NOMINATIONS

1982	1983	1984
Florence Morgan	Dorothy Wheeler	Marjorie Woods

ADMINISTRATIVE BOARD

Stan Perkins, Ch.	Lyle Martin	Mildred Hale
Naoma Perkins	Iva McMichael	Delloise Buchanan
Pearl Martin	Marguerite Ackerman	Lyle Buchanan
John Drlik	Richard Hale	Beverly Post
	Evelyn Stender	Wayne Gilbert
	Althea Ferguson	Ardis McLaren

CHURCH CHANCEL 1982

The Lloyd R. McLaren Family. He passed away in 1970. They are left to right. Bottom row: Marie McLaren Plant, Sue McLaren Hayes, Peggy McLaren Brown. Top row: Mrs. Ardis McLaren, Janet McLaren Burns, Michael L. McLaren, Melissa McLaren.

CHAPTER V

YOUNG PEOPLE

THE MOST VALUABLE ASSET of the (now) Duffield United Methodist Church down this historic road to the present day has been its young people. This is true of most organizations in our society. The promise and strength for the future are in the hands of the young.

Down through the generations this church has been most fortunate. Of late it is suffering. Because of the voluminous records of the Sunday School, Epworth League or M.Y.F. we are lifting samples from each. Conveniently at hand is a report when one John Warren was the Superintendent of Sunday School. It appears that Marian (Post) Newman was Secretary-Treasurer. Teachers could have been Elsie Kerr, Marguerite Gilbert, Iva McMichael, Theo Post and Ardis (Brown) McLaren. Lorna Kenyon could have been their piano player because they paid her $12.50 per month. There was a refreshing young fellow about Duffield, at that time, Don Nemecek, a scion of that steady Drlik Family, whom the Sunday School Treasurer paid 50¢ a week. The only job that fits that wage scale for a date in the fifties would be sanitation engineer. Could he have been the downstairs janitor?

Out of pure nostalgia, here is a run-down from a book entitled "Register of Scholars." That is an almighty important sounding title. It was compiled in the year 1954. Since that time other members have been added.

Ackerman, Frank
Ackerman, Fred
Boist, Arlene
Boist, Walter
Brown, Ardis
Brown, Arthur
Brown, Clara
Brown, Donna
Brown, Ernest
Brown, Robert
Buchanan, Nancy
Buchanan, Sally
Burton, Beulah
Burton, Darwin
Burton, Erwin
Burton, Genevieve
Burton, Katherine
Bush, Lila
Bush, Maxine
Burkowick, Julie
Carrier, Bert
Carrier, Delloise
Carrier, Kathy
Carrier, Janette
Cavil, Verona
Coffield, Joanne
Coffield, Judy
Coffield, Ted
Coffield, Tom
Cuat, Elmer
Drlik, Eva
Drlik, Jane
Drlik, John M.
Drlik, Leslie
Drlik, Vera
DuPraw, Nicole
DuPraw, Ryan
Edwards, Gene
Edwards, Larry
Edwards, Roberta
Frutchey, Janice
Gilbert, Gerald
Gilbert, Janice

Gilbert, Jimmy
Gilbert, Tommy
Gilmore, Ruth
Harris, Eleanor
Harris, Elizabeth
Harris, Willard
Higgins, Forrest
Huff, Betty Ann
Huff, Carolyn
Huff, Mary Lou
Huff, Robert
Huff, Ronald
Jennings, Nancy
Jennings, Phyllis
Jennings, Roger
Kerr, Susie
Kimble, Martin
Kimble, Michael
Lawrence, Ernest
Lobdell, Dallas
Lobdell, Janet
Lobdell, Judy
Lewis, Jimmy
Luce, Helen
Mapes, Florence
Mapes, Maida
McLaren, Bobbie
McLaren, Catherine
McLaren, Don
McLaren, Janet
McLaren, Marie
McLaren, Melissa
McLaren, Michael
McLaren, Norma
McLaren, Peggy
McLaren, Shirley
McLaren, Sue
McMichael, Burdette
McMichael, Ford
McMichael, June
McMichael, Maude
McMichael, Pamela
McMichael, Robert

Middlesworth, Bula
Middlesworth, Evlyn
Middlesworth, George
Middlesworth, Irene
Middlesworth, J. J.
Middlesworth, Merle
Middlesworth, Ray M.
Morgan, Arnold
Morgan, Douglas
Morgan, Larry
Morgan, Martha
Morgan, Wayne
Nemecek, Donald
Nemecek, Jerry
Newman, Danny
Newman, Terry
Newman, Wayne
Nimphie, Clara
Nimphie, Harlow
Nimphie, Laverne
Nimphie, Marjorie
Nimphie, Roy
Parker, Ardonna
Parker, David
Parker, Donald
Parker, Esther
Parker, Robert
Pavlik, Audrey
Pavlik, Bruce
Perkins, Elmer
Perkins, Gertrude
Perkins, Fenton
Pillen, Janene
Pillen, Donna
Pillen, Ronald
Porter, Kenneth
Porter, Mildred
Post, Jerry
Post, John III
Post, Judy
Post, Julie
Post, Karen
Post, Nancy

YOUNG PEOPLE

Post, Patti
Post, Shirley
Post, Tammy
Purdy, Andre
Purdy, Henry
Purdy, Jeff
Purdy, Lee
Purdy, Neal
Purdy, Paul

Purdy, Phillip
Teeter, Dan
Teeter, Mary
Teeter, Randy
Teeter, Shannon
Teeter, Terry
Warren, Gerald
Warren, John Jr.

Warren, Latisha
Warren, Paula
Warren, Thelma
Warren, Verna
Wheeler, Gail
Wheeler, Karen
Wheeler, Nancy
Wheeler, Timothy

BAREFOOTS

*Are these boys playing hookey from Sunday School?
Can you identify them?*

ALL DRESSED UP FOR SUNDAY SCHOOL

The Jennings children, Roger, Phyllis and Nancy, ready for Church and Sunday School on Easter Sunday 1945.

The teenage youth group has switched names rather than fight. It has been changed two or three times but it always comes out the same. They are just as fine a group of country young people as the 4-H'ers. It takes dedicated talent and forward looking people to lead this age group. They have been available. Here are the names of some Chairpersons of that group:

> Donald Ellis   Audrey Pavlik
> Donna Brown   Carolyn Huff
> Ardis Brown   Michael McLaren
> Delloise Carrier   Fred Ackerman

Marguerite Ackerman was Superintendent of the Sunday School for 12 years. Some that have given of their time

DUFFIELD CHURCH YOUTH GROUP, May 1959

The Youth Group at Duffield Methodist in April 1959 as led by Marguerite (Stevens) Ackerman. Those identified are: top row left to right, Fred Ackerman, Daniel Newman. Second row Judy Coil, JoAnn Coffield, Pamela McMichael, Judy Coffield, M. Caswell, Phillip Purdy; bottom row, Paul Purdy, Patricia Post, Norma McLaren, Michael McLaren, James Gilbert.

unselfishly, as teachers, down through the years have been, Florence Morgan, Agnes Jennings, John and Thelma Warren, Lillie Deake, Ruth Burton, Dorothy Wheeler, Marjorie Woods, Muriel Morgan, Joyce Morgan, Marguerite Gilbert, Ardis McLaren and Elsie Kerr, plus a host of others.

The Duffield Church was never the little "church in the valley," nor could it be identified as a church on a "high, high hill." There never was a song composed about it, but many would apply. There was, however, a poem written about the Duffield Church in 1944 by Agnes Jennings and it is reprinted here.

THE DUFFIELD CHURCH

The Duffield Methodist Congregation first came alive
In about the year of eighteen hundred and fifty-five.
They did not have a church building, in which to pray
So, they worshipped at the schoolhouse, on the Sabbath Day.

Through the untiring efforts of a faithful few,
The first Methodist Church came into view.
People came from miles away,
On horseback, wagon and open sleigh.

The building was dedicated in eighteen hundred ninety-one,
In it, many souls for God were won.
Forty-eight years later in nineteen hundred and thirty-nine
A fire destroyed our Church divine.

But it lit a spark of faith and hope,
In the hearts of all the Duffield Folk.
They prayed, planned and worked together,
In sunshine, rain and stormy weather.

In nineteen hundred and forty-one
The new church was finally done.
May it endure for years to come,
As a work of God, a work well done.

                              Agnes Langdon Jennings

Duffield could well be famous for what did not happen within the community rather than for what did. There have been times of stress, some scabrous Halloween pranks and right after the enactment of the Eighteenth Amendment there was a brief period of time when the source of good whisky for medicinal purposes was non-existent. Factionalism and feuding did not have to be controlled because there was none. Difference of opinion was always resolved by open discussion and a decision by the elders or church official board. Any differences of this type were looked upon only as separate ways to arrive at the same end. Personalitites were seldom a factor.

The church has been blessed with a parade of fifty-four officially appointed pastors plus unnumbered supply pastors that

AGNES JENNINGS
Sunday School teacher
and poet

served for short periods. Some of these were mediocre. Others seemed to be tuned to the heartstrings of the community and were released with reluctance. Yet, no great theologians have used the Duffield Church as a springboard.

What then could be the reason for its eminence?

It does not arise from the physical church, because it has always been extremely modest both in exterior appearance and interior furnishings. Prayer meetings were first held in the homes of the early settlers. They used the shelter of a local school and the Gleaner Hall before coming into a home of their own only to lose it back to dust and ashes at the hands of an overheated furnace. It arose again as a tree sprouts forth, after being classified as a hand hewn shrine. So there is nothing physical in consideration here.

It is not the location. Perhaps the reason that the church is on this exact site is because of a gift of land.

The soil could not have had too much influence except that it was a fertile plain, overpopulated with the great hardwoods of oak, maple and ash.

Water quality from bubbling springs and hand dug wells was unique but not to the extent that it had anything to do with the prominence of this House of Worship.

The railroad station, the north and south road that traverses Genesee County, and the settlement derived its name from a renowned man of that era, Dr. Samuel Pearce Duffield. He spent time here and was interested in the chemical properties of the water.

Other tangible assets can be brought to attention that are not as basic as the ones mentioned. Their influence upon this particular church could also be classified as infinitesimal, the same as the above reiterations.

What then is the important factor?

It is the people. In church, people are grouped together and called the congregation. This could be a misnomer. People are the church.

People with deep roots in the Duffield community, residents who became mobile, and recent occupants of a crop of new homes, together with their families comprise this valued ingredient.

We pray that the Duffield United Methodist Church may be perpetuated so that when, in the future, if a stranger asks the question, "Where are you from?", and you answer, with confidence, "Duffield"; the stranger will not respond with a blank stare, but reply, "Yes, everyone knows where Duffield is located. You people are well identified." Let us make it so.

The people of the Duffield Church look forward optimistically to the future.

CHAPTER VI

THE RAILROAD

IF YOU WERE TO PREPARE A GRAPH with two lines, one for railroad activities and the other for business in Duffield, they would follow the same arc. They would parallel each other.

As railroad service came to the countryside it was observed that it was best to build a station about every four to six miles where people had settled. With roads and trails being what they were, that was the maximum distance that could be traveled conveniently to trade in most seasons of the year. In the run from Durand to Flint, depots, freight houses, horse sheds, stockyards and switching sidings were built at Otterburn, Swartz Creek and Duffield with a flag stop at Crapo Farms. This conformed to the pattern.

The linkup between Canada, Port Huron and Chicago was destined to cut the corner of Gaines Township. Note the map on page 46 of a proposed line that died a natural death because of lack of financing and other pressures.

On February 1, 1877 a railroad line was formally opened between Flint and Lansing. It was a beautiful level roadbed that the engineers loved to run. Duffield was at 780 feet above sea level, Crapo Farm 774 feet, Swartz Creek 779 feet and Otterburn 771. It was built by the Chicago & Northeastern Railroad. At Lansing the road joined the Peninsular Railway which connected to the Michigan Central. This now was a continuous line from

FIRST RAILROAD SURVEY LINE 1869-70

The first Railroad Survey line made in 1870 that followed the high ground. This is the line followed by Dr. Duffield. You will note springs designated in several locations.

Port Huron to Chicago. In 1880 these lines were consolidated under the Chicago & Grand Trunk System. 1900 brought about another change of name to Grand Trunk of Canada. By noting the map on page 47 and comparing it with the map on page 46 you will note a route change to provide service to Crapo Farms.

By this time Henry Howland Crapo, who was referred to as former Governor Crapo, had an influence in construction of the Flint and Holly Railroad and it was not difficult for him to secure a relocation of the track to his property, as well as special freight rates from the Vanderbilt Interests who owned the Northeastern. This was not looked upon as unusual or hypocritical in the railroad business of that era.

THE RAILROAD

RAILROAD LINE AS CONSTRUCTED FROM SURVEY OF 1876

A condensed review of railroad scheming about 1850 could be in order here as matter of background. Two struggling railroads pooled their lines and resources on February 13, 1855. They were the Oakland and the Detroit and Pontiac. They became the Detroit and Milwaukee Railway. By the summer of '56 this rail line was extended to Owosso and by the time of the winter freeze up to St. Johns. On July 4, 1856 the first train went through Gaines. Connecting stage lines were run to Byron, Fletchers Corners, Newburgh and Miller Settlement to coincide with the train schedule. This railroad cut the southwest corner of Gaines

Township and provided the first convenient connection for settlers in what was later to be called Duffield, with the outside world.

In another 21 years the railroad was built through Duffield and the following descriptive account details the reason for this delay.

There was a desire that became an obsession, among financiers, to control commerce between Chicago, the East and Canada. The Railroad Conspiracy of 1850 unveiled principals and their goals. It was December 13, 1871 before a multitude of problems could be solved and the railroad became operational from Port Huron to Flint. It was built under the Northern Railroad Bill and called Port Huron & Lake Michigan Railroad. The great International Bridge was completed in 1873 thus making it possible for rail traffic from Michigan to cross Canada via the Grand Trunk to Buffalo and New York.

The Grand Trunk had mentally projected a rail line across Michigan to Chicago in the 1860's. When William H. Vanderbilt bought both the Canada Southern and the Michigan Central, Henry Tyler, President of the Grand Trunk, saw that they would be at the mercy of Vanderbilt between Detroit and Chicago. The game of checkers by these financial wizards was just beginning.

The first segment sought by President Tyler for the Canadian Grand Trunk was from Port Huron to Flint. Another line that Tyler coveted was between Lansing and Battle Creek. That line was completed in '69 by the Peninsular Railway Company. Additional track was laid by the same company on to Valparaiso, Indiana, soon thereafter. Thus the only gap between Chicago and Toronto was the forty-nine miles between Lansing and Flint.

Being an opportunist and of tremendous business acumen, Vanderbilt bought the option. Surveying began in November of '74 under the name of Chicago and Northeastern Railroad Company. Construction was pushed during all of '75 and by the freeze up in '76 the grade was in. It was opened for traffic February 1, 1877 as previously stated. The purpose was to destroy competition by holding forty-nine miles of track and equipment "smack-dab" in the middle of Henry Tyler's Canada to Chicago mainline. The Vanderbilt Combine already had the Port Huron, Detroit, Chicago line tied up.

Tyler secured capital to battle the Vanderbilts by selling an unimportant line in Canada for $1,500,000.00.

He was encouraged by the people of Detroit and wherever else he went in Michigan because there were strong feelings against the Vanderbilt interests over the manner in which they had manipulated the Michigan Central and the Great Railroad Conspiracy of 1850. Everyone wanted to help out with a plan for foiling the Vanderbilts.

The Port Huron to Flint line fell into financial distress because of pressure put on by the Eastern interests sponsored by you know who. Vanderbilt made an offer to the bondholders to redeem the company. It was so low that Tyler was sought out for a bid. No offer was tendered. On June 27, 1879 that railroad was put up at auction. The Canadian Grand Trunk bid $300,000.00 and "the hammer fell before the Vanderbilt emissary could utter a word." The auctioneer was in control and there was no doubt where his sympathy lay. Grand Trunk pressed on by buying up the bonds of the three Peninsular sections westward of Lansing for as little as twelve cents on a dollar.

Thus with both ends of the Canada Chicago route safely in the bag they began a diversional tactic on the eastern capitalists by surveying another route between Flint and Lansing to pass through Corunna and Owosso.

Thereupon, William Vanderbilt offered to sell his middle section from Lansing through Duffield to Flint for $600,000.00, about one half of the construction cost. The transfer was consummated shortly thereafter for $540,000.00.

James M. Turner of Lansing who had actually built the Chicago & Northeastern for Vanderbilt profited the most from these dealings. This is the condensed story of the development of the Grand Trunk Western Railway as the mainline of the Canadian National in the heartland of the United States.

Duffield was on line. Bringing the story of the railroad from the field of international finance and intrigue down to the local level is what would be called a "giant step" in the old one room country school game of "May I."

Michigan's first settlements were located beside the waterways. These waterways provided easy access to the interior areas but by extended indirect routes. On the contrary, railroads were

HIGHBALLING OUT OF DUFFIELD STATION

Train service opened up the back country to trade and commerce. Note the number of mail and baggage cars in this Grand Trunk fast train. From the Brian Osmer collection

the shortest distance between two points. A second series of towns took root beside these bands of steel. They grew like mushrooms as the result of railroad service. Among them was Duffield.

This first depot, illustrated on page 51, was constructed before the first train rolled in 1877. It was located on the northwest quadrant of the crossing on ground level with the roadbed. The Carrier barn, outbuildings and farm machinery make up the backdrop.

This first station was built by the Vanderbilts and conformed to the style and size they had standardized. It was a better quality station than the later station built by the Grand Truck Western on the opposite side of the tracks and of Duffield Road. The reason for the change or the fate of this first beautiful station is unknown at this writing, except for a hearsay rumor which was passed down from a previous generation. It went something like this.

VANDERBILT DEPOT

Duffield's first depot built before the line was put into operation, February 1, 1877. Carrier farm buildings in background.

A man by the name of Pat Delano had set up a sawmill across the road from the depot. It was steam powered with the slab wood and scraps being used to fuel the boiler. Sparks from this sawmill were said to have ignited some waste materials piled behind the depot and the fire was quite advanced before anyone noticed the blaze.

The only fire quencher available then was the human bucket brigade and the water had to be drawn by bucket or pumped by hand. Regardless, the fine first depot was a total loss.

This account is without substantiation so it will not be mentioned.

Economically the railroad was a source of employment. The depot agent was a local kingpin. He dressed in the official railroad uniform that was a semi-military dark blue with his title embossed on the cap. He was regarded with awe by the youngsters. The adults looked on him as their confidant. He was

DEPOT FOR THE DURATION

This replacement depot was built in 1908 on the southeast quadrant of the Duffield crossing. It was a high ceiling frame building set on pilings. The dimensions were 14 by 38 feet with an extended overhang to protect passengers and freight from the elements. Records verify that there were also a stockyard and outhouse. Grand Trunk Western discontinued use of the depot for passenger service in 1931. The building was moved to the Durand Yards in 1939 and served as a tool house. "A 1917 comprehensive inventory indicated the building was worth $1,226.00, the furniture and platform $480.00, the stockyard $283.00 and the outhouse $350.00."

This information was furnished by John David Williams, Vice President of Public Relations for the Grand Trunk. The writer willingly accepts the above appraisals with one exception. The value placed on the outhouse was inflated.

sworn to secrecy. Only he knew to what destination they had bought a ticket for last Saturday night. Only he knew what message they had paid for to be sent out by Morse Code over the telegraph wire or what they had received in return. All the important personal news came by way of the depot agent including births, deaths, business transactions and so on. In a country station he was also the freight agent and responsible for seeing that the mail was delivered safely to the post office. When business boomed on the railroad, stations were manned twenty-four hours per day. The shifts were called "tricks" and were called the first, second and third "trick." Some of the depot agents at Duffield were:

Mr. Carlson	Clinton Nimphie
Floren Thomas	Arthur Brown
George Perkins	George Martin

Jobs were available for other local people on the railroad. Emil Buta, the father of Stanley and John, worked on the tracks. John Nemecek, Sr. worked on the section. Albert Clark was the

THE ESSENTIAL LOCAL FREIGHT

This local freight could have been in Duffield to switch the last load of sugar beets of the season over on the main line for delivery to Owosso.

Local freight trains stopped twice each day. Engine 1620 was an early caller. From the Brian Osmer collection

THE STEAMER ENGINE 2681

THE STEAMER ENGINE 5632

Engine 2681 and 5632 that often polished the rails on the main line through Duffield. From the Brian Osmer collection

section foreman and Frank Tranzow was track superintendent. These last two were the ones to contact if you were looking for a job. Many men about Duffield worked on the railroad for short periods, but did not make a career of it. A. J. Ferguson, who was raised near town, is presently Yard Superintendent at Flint.

Ralph Parker was raised by the Henry Nimphie Family beside the tracks, in what is now the Dale Jenkins Place. The Nimphie Boys were Harlow, Clinton, Patrick and Michael. All of them were, at some time during their lives, involved with the Grand Trunk. Ralph Parker played in the hay sheds, climbed the stockyard fence and watched them grade and lay the double track.

The work gang consisted of two hundred men recruited by contract out of Chicago. They lived in bunk cars on the Duffield siding while building several miles of track both ways from the station. It was a self-contained unit.

The lasting impressions that have remained with Ralph were about the food, the cook's arbors and the evening camp fires. The local passenger train left several burlap bags at the depot each day full of large loaves of black rye bread. Portions were cut from these loaves by the cook holding them under his arm. Wood barrels of salt pork, weighing five hundred pounds each, were rolled off at the freight dock once a week. There was some cured meat but it was mostly what was called fatback. This was supplemented with piles of one hundred pound bags of dry beans. The food was basic and plentiful.

The cook and his helpers were an important element. They built an arbor beside the tracks to fit a sheet iron oven and the large cast iron kettles in which the cooking was done, rain or shine. The cook's helpers also worked as water boys for the crew during working hours.

They congregated around the several camp fires in the evening, according to the language spoken. There was much camaraderie displayed. Singing of folk songs continued for hours, especially on Saturday nights. Sunday was a day off and wash day. Everyone washed his own clothes. They were draped over the railroad fence for extended distances up and down the track to dry. All of this was observed by little Ralph Parker at trackside in Duffield.

HALPIN SCHOOL 1906

Front Row: Myrt Smith, Emmett Griffin, Russell Evans, Sylvester Griffin, Joseph Smith, Leo Halpin, Harry Bemis, Winifred Simpson, Helen Luce, and Rose Griffin. Second Row: Floyd Evans, Art Smith, Frank M. Halpin, Frank Smith, John Halpin, Owen Evans, Frank Griffin, Ernest Evans, and Martin Griffin. Back Row: Jesse Lone (teacher), Ruth Colbrath Burton, Rosie Evans, Florence Mapes, Josephine Luce, Maggie Griffin, and Maida Mapes.

CHAPTER VII

ONE-ROOM SCHOOLS

THERE NEVER WAS A SCHOOL ON THE CROSSROADS in Duffield. However, it enjoyed the activities of three schools. Doane School or East Duffield was less than a mile to the east. North Duffield was one mile to the north and the Halpin School one mile to the south and a quarter of a mile east. There was always considerable rivalry between these local one room country schools.

The Halpin School was legally identified as Gaines School District No. 6. The records were lost when the Herb Frutchey Building was destroyed by fire June 6, 1943. However, some random entries were found in the records of the Village of Gaines:

Insurance on Halpin Schoolhouse	1892	$1.26
Rec'd by School from Twp. Treas	1893	8.61
Paid Mae Halpin Teaching winter term 4 months	1894	100.00
Paid J. C. Luce, Teachers wages, 1 mo.	1896	30.00
Cash on hand to start school	1897	8.86
Paid Seymon Carrier, Teachers wages 1 month	1898	30.00
Paid to Josie Terry for use of well 1 year	1899	2.00
Paid W. B. Cozadd Hdwe. for paint	1900	8.34
Paid Fred J. Moore, Teachers wages 1 month	1905	40.00

Paid for lamps and extra chimney	1906	.74
Library money received	1908	4.14
Vida Lawcock, Teaching 1 month	1911	35.00
Paid Ruth Colbrath, balance on organ	1915	3.75

School was discontinued at the Halpin School with the year 1921.

Some of the other teachers, not mentioned above were, Mary Hynes, Ella Short, Mildred McCann and Jesse Lone.

Taxes for the Halpin School are recorded as being assessed in 1869.

The other two district boundaries split the town. Children on the west side of the road attended North Duffield. Those on the east side went to the Doane. The possibility of conflict in dates of the main activities such as Christmas exercises, box socials, and

NORTH DUFFIELD SCHOOL 1894

Elizabeth Burleson, Teacher. Known pupils are: Robert Herrick, second from left in bottom row, Fenton C. Perkins with cape, Elmer S. Perkins and Charles Derby. Note the broken windows and button shoes.

ONE ROOM SCHOOLS 59

NORTH DUFFIELD SCHOOL 1921

Back row left to right: Eleanor Harris, Harry Woods, Carl Post, Leda Nemecek, Kenneth Porter, Clyde Woods, Ford McMichael, Helen Woods, Mary Hromek, Teacher, Beatrice Perry (Syring)

Front row left to right: George Buta, William Ackerman, John Buta, Frank Nemecek, Stanley Buta, Frank Minarik, Stacia O'Kenka, Mamie Tahalka, Bessie Woods, Josie O'Kenka, Frances O'Brien, Anne Gurica, Maude McMichael, Florence Woods.

Different windows are broken 26 years later.

the likes had to be watched. Everyone in Duffield went to social activities held by all three.

That North Duffield ball team was a hard one to beat. They would take on the Doane School for a warm-up then go over to the Ryno School and beat them good, usually about 20 to 2. At one time the North Duffield team had Ford McMichael, Kenneth

NORTH DUFFIELD SCHOOL ABOUT 1926

1st row: Agnes Cajka, Wayne Gilbert, Mary Buta
2nd row: Josie Okenka, Mary Cajka, Leda Nemecek, Annie Kala, Annie Gurcia, Stacia Okenka, Mary Cesar
3rd row: Dorothy Bowler, Bertha Woods, Marian Post, Catherine Ackerman, Elaine Gilbert, Burdette McMichael, Clare Post, Joe Cesar, John Haist jr.
4th row: Eleanor Harris, Bessie Woods, Maude McMichael, Billy Ackerman, George Buta, Curtis Kranz, John Buta, Frank Minarik, Stanley Buta
5th row: Leda Nemecek, Mary Kala, Adeline Minarik, Florence Woods, Frank Nemecek, Kenneth Porter
6th row: Bernice Williams (Brown), teacher, Nina Woods, Beth Haist, Clyde Woods.

Forty pupils now with some noticeable improvements to the school building.

Porter, George, John and Stan Buta, Harry and Clyde Woods, Carl Post, Frank Nemecek plus a few good spares. They were tough.

Teaching in those schools was a challenge for a teacher. Wages were low, responsibilities were high, but the rewards were worth all the trouble. It was much easier to teach the girls than it was the boys. The boys had so many distractions. When spring broke it was difficult to keep them in school. The enrollment of girls was always the majority and they stayed for the term.

There was only one "hand me down" incident that took place at one of these institutions of learning that was not complimentary. This writer will not even identify the school. The teacher was young and male. I will call him Percy. It was the last day of the winter term. The boys (or I should say men) attended the one room country school until they were 21 years old during the short winter term and there had been some pairing off.

Percy, the teacher, had been fussing with the older girls. Some of them were receiving special attention over and above what would be classified as teaching. One in particular had taken his eye and he had been seeing her home each night by giving her a ride in his buggy. These farm boys did not like that because they were a lookin' too. So—that last day they antagonized the well-dressed romantic Percy to the extent that he asked them to stay in the last recess. He played right into their plans. Dapper Percy turned his back on the disenchanted boys to erase the blackboard. This was a mistake. They jumped him in unison. They shoved him into the corner, beat him with the chalk erasers until his dark suit was all white, tore his coat sleeve, broke his spectacles, crashed a slate down over his head so that it hung about his neck and threw him out the schoolhouse window, much to the surprise of the girls and other younger children that were playing in the yard. The winter term was over an hour and a half early. Teacher Percy did not come back for the next term.

On a Sunday, February 5, 1961, one Kenneth B. Moore wrote a feature article that was published in the *Flint Journal* with the heading, "Five One-Room Schoolhouses Left in County." It featured the Doane School of Duffield. The North Duffield was

DOANE SCHOOL IN SESSION 1961

one of the remaining four. The article is reproduced here in part with the permission of the *Flint Journal*. He says it well.

Learning Process Is Just as Sound, Teacher Contends
Five One-Room Schoolhouses Left in County
By KENNETH B. MOORE

A tradition in American education—the one-room school district—still is very much with us.

True, annexations and consolidations through the years have greatly reduced the number of tiny school districts supporting the one-building, one-classroom and one-teacher type of school system, which once predominated.

Because of the trend toward sprawling halls of learning, most city-dwellers regard "the little red schoolhouse" as a thing of the past.

But tucked away in the farmlands of Genesee County, however, are five such schools. They are in the school districts of Beebe, Doane, Kerr, North Duffield and Stanley.

These districts are self-governing. They are autonomous, like any other district in the county. Their boards of education, which must be the smallest governing units existing are composed of three members each.

The educators at these schools are superintendents, principals and teachers, all rolled into one. The schools have an average enrollment of only 22. The children are in grades ranging from kindergarten through the eighth.

Insignificant as these school districts may seem, they represent what once was the heart of education. They are living monuments to our heritage.

Doane is situated in a section of Gaines Township. Its small, white school stands on Reid Road just east of Nichols Road.

Children had pushed the various-sized desks to the sides of the classroom and were playing a game when I arrived.

Good-natured and robust laughter of the 22 children filled the room as their teacher, Mrs. Hazel Hoffman, proudly told me about her school.

She explained that Doane does not have all the "frills" to be found in city schools but that the learning process is just as sound.

"We're a big, happy family," she said.

Mrs. Hoffman explained that teaching is on more of a personal basis and that it is not uncommon for parents of the children to drop in and spend most of a day at the school.

Interrupting our conversation, she stroked a small desk bell to end recess. In a twinkling, the children had the desks back in place and were back at their studies.

"The children here are well-mannered and delightful to work with," she went on with a smile.

Because Doane children spend kindergarten and their first six grades in the one-room schoolhouse, she said, they form relationships that become nearly brotherly and sisterly.

They look out for each other's welfare, she said. After they go to Durand to complete their schooling, many return on days off to visit with their younger friends at Doane during school hours.

The situation is similar at North Duffield, where Mrs. Betty Williams is in charge of 25 pupils.

The schoolhouse, constructed near Hill and Duffield Roads in 1890, is 30 years older than Doane but bears a marked resemblance.

As is the custom of most teachers in primary school districts, Mrs. Williams instructs the three or four children in one grade while the other grades are busy on previously assigned work.

It is not uncommon for her to be helping one child in spelling and being interrupted several times by a fourth-grader asking about a geography question or a fifth-grader seeking explanation of a history lesson.

"Flexibility is the key for rural teachers." she chuckled.

The children who attend these schools have a certain freshness and courtesy which do credit to their teachers and parents.

Most of the students are neat as a pin and the desktops, although showing wear, are relatively unmarred.

And the children appear to enjoy their school experience. A fifth-grader said: "When it's time to play, we have fun. And when our teacher says to work, that's what we do."

The teachers will tell you that they are firm believers in this kind of education and that they enjoy being the entire staff.

"We work out our own problems, make our own decisions and the children respect this," said one.

"Teaching in this type of a situation offers a real challenge," said another, "and the rewards become as great as the challenge."

The length of time remaining for the one-room school district is in doubt, however, as several of the teachers pointed out.

They noted, with not a little sadness, that the world is catching up with the little red schoolhouse, and each wonders if hers will be the next to go.

They point out that not too long ago there were many such school districts in the county.

And no matter how strongly the cause of the little red schoolhouse has been or is defended, they said, this fact remains:

Now there are only five.

As the years have accrued, the desire for education has surged to the extent that the facilities have, at times, been taxed to capacity. This was not so in the formative years of the Duffield Community. Few young men completed the eighth grade at the local one room school. The reasoning that prevailed was that a strong back was more valuable than an educated mind. There never seemed to be time for both.

For a few decades this held the upper hand and then values began to assume a gradual but definite direction in favor of education.

Upon the successful completion of eight grades in the country school and the passing of a state examination, a student was

DOANE SCHOOL, May 1911

Front Row—Jason Allen, Howard O'Brien, John Hynes, Charlie Whitney, Leona Thomas, Margaret Hynes, Mildred Whitney, Lorna McCaughna.

2nd Row—Bertha O'Brien, Bill O'Brien, Paul O'Brien, Walter McCaughna, Raymond Hynes, Willard Allen, Mae Brown, Harold Allen

3rd Row—Floyd Brown, Carl Hynes, Beatrice Barker, Agnes Curtis, Jeanette McCaughna, Elizabeth O'Brien

Back Row—George Conroy, Homer Whitney, Jessie Hardick, Henry Hartwell, Julia O'Brien, Gertrude Allen, Marie O'Brien, Cash Curtis, Teacher.

Picture named by Elizabeth O'Brien Stevenson

granted entrance into one of several local high schools. The tuition was paid by the student's local district to the high school of entry. Few scholarships were available toward a college or university degree. It was a "nip and tuck" battle for many deserving students and most were unable to achieve their personal goals. Then along came progress.

It is gratifying for one in the background, who has lived during this era, to observe the status of the educational opportunities presently available. No student or adult seeking knowledge needs to pass through this life without exercising his potential.

DOANE SCHOOL—1924

Doane School 1924 with a former student of the Halpin School as teacher. They are bottom row left to right: Charles Moticka, John Moticka, Joe Drlik, Anna Jancar, Helen Burton, Bessie Moticka, John Jancar.

Second row: Carl Richardson, Arlene Boist, Helen Drlik, Christine Martin, Ruth Leonard, Anna Hudy.

Third row: Frank Drlik, Robert Holcomb, Ethel Barker, Joe Moticka, Emil Drlik.

Top row: Dorothy Jancar, Teacher Ruth Burton, Catherine Drlik.

CHAPTER VIII

VILLAGE AND ADJACENT BUSINESSES

OVERTOWN, UPTOWN, DOWNTOWN, all put you in town at Duffield. It never was a complete entity. The have nots were: barbershop, saloon, doctor and restaurant. Now! Those are a lot of important have nots.

The haves were: a church, railroad, depot, elevator, stockyard, 3 sugar beet sub-stations, post office, general stores, Gleaner Hall, blacksmith shops, cider mill, jelly factory, brick and tile kiln, cement block plant, implement dealer, gas stations, Watkins Dealer, Owls Nest and maybe a bootlegger.

By scanning these various businesses that were in Duffield, it is rational to conclude that the surrounding agriculture was the beckoning hand. Various plat maps printed herein contain the names of the early settlers. Descendants of these people now occupy the land or are still living in the vicinity. For some undiscernable reason most of the Irish families acquired land on the south side of Reid Road with only a couple exceptions. Those who hailed from the land of Erin and were registered as early landowners were:

Michael and Nellie O'Brien	Patrick Clune
Timothy and Agnes O'Brien	Thomas Conroy
James and Ella O'Brien	Daniel Dolehanty
Edward Burns	John Dolehanty

Michael and Elizabeth Halpin
Edward M. Hynes
George Hynes
John and Bridget Hynes
John Paul Hynes
Terrence Hynes
Perry Hynes
Patrick Martin
Michael O'Dea
Edward Burns

The present family name Delehanty, prominent within the area, is a fracture of the original Dolehanty. These families established "Little Corktown" of Gaines Township. The first to come were Michael and Ellen Halpin from Tipperary, Ireland in 1857. Because of the good reports they sent back, the others soon followed.

Catholicism was begun in the area by traveling missionaries. By 1871 St. Joseph Catholic Church, with the support of many

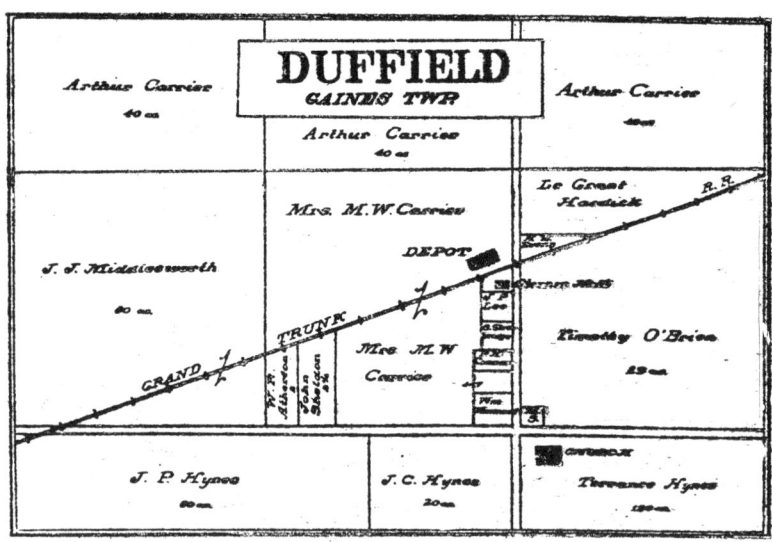

A CORNER OF GAINES TOWNSHIP

A corner map of Gaines Township taken from Standard Atlas of Genesee County, Michigan, George A. Ogle & Co., 1905, showing Reid Road as somewhat of a demarcation line for "Little Corktown."

TWO LADIES OF THE HYNES CLAN

Irish settlers from the Duffield area and Father Joseph Kramer, was established in Gaines as a mission out of Fenton.

Father Leo Talbot was reared in the area. His mother was a sister to Patrick Delehanty. Cleland Dolehanty also assumed the priesthood. Dolehanty and Delehanty were synonymous, one branch of the family decided to use the "e" for identification purposes. The following Catholic young women became Sisters: Anna Dolehanty, M. Placidia and Esther Halpin, also Celia, Josephine and Vera Burns.

The Gleaners were a strong organization that built a substantial hall in Duffield right "smack-dab" up against the south side of the tracks on the west side of the road. People came from far and wide to attend meetings of this lodge. Because it was located on a mainline railroad in central Michigan it was the scene of many district and state meetings of the Gleaners Lodge and Insurance Company.

CARO, MICHIGAN.   JULY 25, 1896.   VOL. 2—NO. 10

⇥ NO ASSESSMENT FOR AUGUST. ⇤

MORE SUBSTANTIAL PROOF.

YOU have undoubtedly heard wise ones discuss the question of risks in Fraternal societies, and many of them have claimed that there was no difference between the risks incurred in granting endowment certificates to men engaged in any of the many pursuits, outside the hazardous occupations. The Ancient Order of Gleaners has claimed from its inception that it was unfair to class men of all occupations under one assessment rate, and the reports of every society thus far have proven the assertion. In the report of Great Record Keeper Watson, to the last meeting of the Great Camp, K. O. T. M., held at Saginaw, we find some valuable proof to substantiate the claims made by the Ancient Order of Gleaners.

Great Record Keeper Watson says: "The following table shows the different occupations in which the membership is engaged and the death rate per thousand in each:"

Occupation	Death Rate per 1,000
Attorneys	5.37
Agents	14.96
Bakers	7.04
Butchers	23.35
Cabinet Makers	6.90
Electricians	19.23
Engineers	7.01
Firemen	6.00
Harness Makers	8.77
Liquor Dealers	30.65
Lumbermen	11.23
Manufacturers	5.38
Machinists	5.30
Merchants	6.08
Millers	5.30
Mill Operators	8.73
Painters	6.91
Physicians and Dentists	6.28
Printers	5.10
Sailors	13.94
Street Car Employees	19.41
Stone Cutters	19.41
Telegraphers	8.88
Traveling Salesmen	12.99
Miscellaneous	5.30
Farmers	**4.14**

There were thirty nine occupations given and among them were eleven occupations with lower rate than the farmer, and among these were ministers and school teachers, both of whom are eligible to membership in the Ancient Order of Gleaners. If we combine the thirty eight occupations and figure the death rate we have the following:

Average death rate per 1,000 members of all occupations except farmers 7.47
Average Death Rate of Farmers, per 1,000 .... 4.14
In favor of the Farmer, per 1,000 members 3.33

This table certainly shows that it is a rank injustice to those engaged in agriculture to be classed with other occupations in the matter of figuring assessment rates for death benefits. When we take the above and figure it out in dollars and cents, we find still greater evidence to prove that the farmer can save money by uniting with those engaged in the same occupation. The Ancient Order of Gleaners is the first society in the world to limit its endowment membership to the agriculturists of the world, and its record has certainly proven the wisdom of this feature of the Order.

When you are soliciting members for the Order among your farmer friends it would be well to remember these figures and present them for his consideration. Certainly the experience of older societies should govern the younger ones, and if such experience results beneficial to the younger Orders they are at liberty to profit thereby.

———

The Prize Banner will be awarded soon after the 15th of August. In sending in the names of new members be sure and give full name and policy number. Remember the work of sending in the names is to be done by the Local Secretaries. The State Arbor has nothing to do with the reports and only those who send in the names will be considered in the contest.

TO-DAY'S DUTY.

"In to-day walks to-morrow."
To-morrow, then, depends upon to-day. There is no guess work about it. Nothing "happens." Effects follow causes in all things. It is true that the causes are not always discoverable, but that does not alter the fact. To-day we train for to-morrow's test. The babe coos that the child may talk; the boy builds bridges of matches that the man may span rivers.

If the young man is not "ready for business" to-day, can he be sure that he will be to-morrow? The emergency of the next day may come before he is ready for it. Then he will say, "If I had only prepared myself yesterday!" Here is the Biblical question, a true answer to which will forcibly impress the idea which we wish to convey: "If thou hast run with the footmen, and they have wearied thee, how then canst thou contend with horses?" The application of the principle may be made with another question: How can the young man who slights the small duty expect to safely bear the great responsibility?

We are altogether too willing to put off the day of preparation until the day we should be fully prepared. It is easy to say, "I'll attend to that some other time," not realizing that the "other time" may be upon us almost before we know it. This lack of courage to make present duties and opportunities and sacrifices contribute to to-morrow's strength explains many failures. A brave young man who is sensible enough to judge something of the future by the past will endure the burdens and disappointments of the present for the sake of the future; as an oarsman grows weary in the toil of training in order that he may win the pennant. Burdens to-day need not be burdensome to-morrow; disappointment to-day means success to-morrow if only a man have the right kind of stuff in him.

"In to-day walks to-morrow."

Village And Adjacent Businesses

It was a combination fraternal and business organization of which there were many at that time. A local Gleaner organization, as was in Duffield, was called an Arbor. Their ritual was taken from the Biblical story of Ruth. Local officers were Chief Gleaner, Secretary, Conductor, Treasurer, Chaplain, Inner Guard, Outer Guard and Supreme Council. In initiation, a recruit had to ride a goat around the hall. The State Arch published a monthly magazine. The front page from the July 26, 1896 issue is reproduced with permission of the Gleaner Life Insurance Company, Bill Warner, Executive Vice President, Adrian, Michigan. At one time there were 246 arbors the same as the "Golden Rod Arbor" in Duffield. Everyone belonged. It was also the center of all social activity, especially of the church.

Within Duffield, which we have called a typical U.S. agricultural oriented community, the development of business trailed along behind education and socializing. It began with the basics and not businesses as we list them today in the yellow pages. These businesses were necessary if the settlers stayed put. To stay put was another way of saying, "We have food, shelter and clothing to make it until we can bring in the next crop."

One of these essential businesses that serviced the farmers was the blacksmith. Duffield, at one time, had two. One we must name the ghost shop, because it has been positively identified by two oldtimers. It was opposite the depot where the remains of the elevator now stand. It was in a shacky lean-to and the smithy's name is unknown.

Kitty-wampus to the church was a solid establishment run for years by William Merchant. It has been stated that he was a short square built man who would not tolerate foolishness from man or beast and could repair anything that was fixable, build anything that was needed, and put shoes on the worse tempered mustang they could ship into Duffield from the western prairie.

If he was in a good mood he would allow the town boys to come into his shop and run the bellows. If not, they knew how to keep their distance out in the street where they could still watch the sparks fly. As he grew older he mellowed and everyone called him Uncle Billy Merchant. He was considered the town's craftsman of that day.

THE MIDDLESWORTH FACTORY

J. J. Middlesworth, Manufacturer of Brick and Tile, Wholesale and Retail, Duffield, Michigan

These sheds that are running both ways from the main building were for air drying the wet tile before they were wheeled into the kiln. The kiln is the dome-shaped structure in the middle. In the background there is another smokestack, this was for the upright steam engine that powered the plant. The fence in the foreground is the railroad right-of-way fence. Two men have been positively identified by Howard Atherton. Second from the left is William R. Atherton, his father. Sam Hudson is fourth from the left, the tall man in the dark clothing.

One of the great places of interest in Duffield was the tile and brick yard. A clay pit was opened on the north side of Reid Road just beyond the railroad and Jones Creek. This clay contained a generous portion of ferrous oxide. When properly fired it made nicely colored red brick and tile. John J. Middlesworth was the most capable owner and operator.

The main source of power at the yards was an upright steam engine in which they burned coal. The power it produced was harnessed for several tasks.

One of the tasks allocated to the upright steam engine was to winch clay from the pit to the grinding and molding shed with a cable attached to a one yard cart. This cart was pulled upgrade out of the mine on a narrow gauge steel track. It was on four steel wheels about the size of the wheels on an old-fashioned railroad handcar. The sides of the cart were four feet high and it was eight feet long. The cart was loaded by hand with pick and shovel. It had a side dump. When empty it was returned to the pit by gravity. It had a habit of jumping the track if it was allowed to return downgrade too fast.

This same steam engine was also used to mix the clay and run a water hydraulic ram that pressed the clay through the molds. As it came from the molds the material, either tile or brick shape, was cut by hand into proper lengths. The power was transferred from one shaft to the other by a series of belts that were switched from drive to idle pulleys as the power was needed for the various operations.

At one time, Charles Hudson, Enos Kenyon, William Atherton and Sam Hudson were the crew. In the transferring of power from one operation to another, Charlie Hudson's arm became entangled in a couple of those leather belts. That steam engine had no soul, no brain and no conscience. It just kept on chugging and shooting black smoke from the stack. It nearly tore Charlie's arm off at the elbow. They made a tourniquet of leather belt lacing that they twisted up tight with a piece of broken shovel handle, to stop the loss of blood. They gave Charlie all the good whisky they could get down him and called Doctor Haviland from Lennon. Haviland had the fastest horse in the area.

The Doctor arrived in less than thirty minutes followed by about everyone else on the road or who had a horse handy. It took three strong men to hold Hudson while the Doctor squared off the splintered bone with a common hand saw which was used about the place, and sewed the skin over the remaining stub of an arm. Charles Hudson lived and did not suffer any major infection from this painful ordeal.

John J. Middlesworth also operated a cider mill and an apple jelly making factory with about the same machinery, in season. They used the same hydraulic water press to squeeze the cider from the ground apples. They would make boiled apple juice,

Middlesworth's Windmill

SIMPLE, CHEAP and DURABLE

There's money in this for you

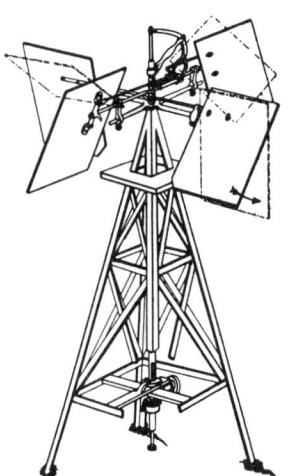

Invented by JNO. J. MIDDLESWORTH of Duffield, Mich.

he above cut shows a new and improved form of windmill of simple construction, that is durable, and in which the objectionable features in other mills are done away with

It will be noted that the wind wheel is hung over the center of the tower, thereby reducing to a minimum the strain placed upon the tower during the operation of the mill

The fan blades are so constructed that they govern the speed of the mill, being pivotally hung on the arms, as shown, they present a surface to the wind up to a certain speed; a faster revolution would not give the blades time to drop by the time it could be acted upon by the wind. The dotted lines, showing the position of the blade as it passes out of direct contact with the wind, will enable the reader to understand this. The mill is thus prevented from racing, and thus impairing its usefulness, as well as that of any connected machinery.

When it is desired to put the mill out of operation, the operator will grasp the rod which projects below the lower framework close to the ground, and push up on it giving it a slight turn, which will cause all the blades to present an edge to the wind, so that it will not run no matter how hard the wind blows.

The mill is easy running, requires no attention, is ball bearing, is easily put into or out of operation, has no strain on the tower. It is attractive in appearance, has great power, and perfect governing means. Storms and sudden shifts of the wind cannot harm it.

The mill costs but half to make and put up, as any other now known, and has none of the defects of the others. Its neat appearance, cheapness and durability as well as its mechanical pefection recommend it to all who see it.

This valuable invention is fully protected by a strong U. S. Patent, of recent issue, and is for sale either outright or on royalty and on most reasonable terms. For particulars, model, etc., address:

UNION PATENT INVESTMENT CO......DETROIT. MICHIGAN.

VILLAGE AND ADJACENT BUSINESSES 75

that would not ferment and go into apple jack or vinegar, by using the steam hose from the boiler of the engine for the heat.

Customers would bring their crocks, some as large as fifty gallon, to put their apple jelly in. This took a little more time than the pressing of the cider. Pulp from the various batches of cider, pressed during the day, would be dumped into piles along the tracks from the same cart used to transport the clay. A stake would be stuck in each pile with the owners name written on it for identification. At night, or in spare time, these pulp piles would be worked over and pressed once more. The resulting heavier liquid would be run into open ended oak barrels, sugar added and boiled with steam until such time as it would congeal, when cooled, into apple jelly. Imagine 50 gallons of jelly or even 10. It was a staple sweetner and used for many country cooking purposes.

Customers came from miles around to John J's business which included the tile yard, brick kiln, cider mill and jelly making plant.

The steady non-seasonal business that attracted the populace to Duffield was provided by trading at the General Stores. There were two major and several lesser ones at various times.

William Lamb (also one of the early postmasters) operated a store that was located 10 feet south of the aforementioned Gleaner Hall. In case of fire at either place both would have gone up in smoke. William R. Atherton, who had been a boss at the Middlesworth operation, bought this business from Lamb. William R. was the father of Howard C. Atherton who was born on Reid Road in the first house west of the corner in 1903. This house was later sold to John Nemecek, Sr.

A NEWFANGLED WINDMILL

The engineering problems presented by the combination business of a tile yard, brick factory, sawmill, cider mill and jelly making factory were not enough of a challenge to Jno. J. Middlesworth of Duffield, Mich., as attested by this tear sheet from a Patent Catalogue.

ATHERTON'S GENERAL STORE

Atherton Store with a portion of the Gleaner Hall (center of all community activities) visible in the right background.

People in this picture are left to right: Loren Atherton; Howard Atherton; W. Edgar Atherton, small child; William R. Atherton, Storekeeper; Julia A. Atherton, wife; George Haskell, Drummer (salesman).

Note egg cases and cream cans on porch, hitching posts by the road and coal oil yard lamp on post to the right.

It seems that the Athertons operated a grocery wagon on various routes in the country every Tuesday, Wednesday, Thursday and Friday. A span of bay geldings named Prince and Fred, that were purchased from Frank Hynes, supplied the power. Age caught up with this fine team, after a few years, and they were replaced by a Model T touring car. Ben Hillaker and Rufus Gilbert custom built a trailer to hook behind the Model T to add capacity. The trailer was loaded with staple groceries, such as fresh ground coffee, tea, spices, salt, sugar, flour, cheese, dried fruits, cured meats, salted fish, soda, baking powder, extracts, etc. It was really a portable trading post. Eggs were the most

AT THE DEPOT WITH A CAN OF CREAM

A matured Loren Atherton and Clara Nimphie, daughter of Henry Nimphie, all dressed up in their Sunday best waiting for the fast train to stop and pick up the cream and maybe them too. Could they have been going to the city for a show? They appear to be in a holiday mood.

prominent item of barter. Farm commodities such as live poultry, maple syrup, maple sugar, garden produce, cured meats, plus handcrafted articles and even services were traded in at the grocery wagon for staples that were needed by country people. This Lamb-Atherton Store remained in business until 1916.

The main Trading Post was located on the northeast corner of the Duffield-Reid Road intersection. It was built in 1903 by one Archie Scott and sold in 1904 to Miner S. "Peck" Snow and Charles J. Killeen. The store was stocked with merchandise and opened for business. "Peck" Snow married Veva Beers on

THE NEW STORE

The new store, neat and clean, opened by Miner S. Snow and Charles J. Killeen

November 23, 1904 and they moved into the living quarters above the store. Mr. Killeen sold out his interest to Snow in 1905 and moved to Flint where his descendants reside today. A grocery wagon from this store also went out early each morning to the countryside.

Harry Hardick, son of LeGrant Hardick, worked in this store from the time he was 12 years old. His big job was hand grinding coffee beans each day so there would be a fresh supply for the grocery wagon come morning.

A daughter, Herthyl A. Snow was born above the store December 17, 1907. She is now Mrs. Ray Withey of Flint. In 1910 "Peck" Snow sold his Duffield store to Fred Curtis of Durand. When the Snows moved to Flint, Harry Hardick went with them. He was 17 years of age.

Within less than a year Arthur G. Carrier took over. He became a typical country storekeeper. His business in Duffield was a parallel to Greenfield Village, Dearborn, Michigan. Food staples, dry goods, hardware, oil and gas, farm machinery, mail, party telephones in four exchanges, a lively political discussion, paying prices for all farm produce from parsnips to live geese and choice morsels of local gossip were all readily available. For the sake of the present generation and all those destined to follow we will detail or fan out the last all inclusive sentence. It can be defined as early Americana.

Food staples pertained to flour, corn meal, sugar and salt in bulk, by the barrel, or at least in 100 pound bags. The same was true in dry goods. The material came in bolts 36 or 45 inches wide and was the makings only. The customer took it home and made whatever, out of it. Manufactured items of clothing were almost non-existent. A ribbon could be purchased for milady's hair, a whalebone staved corset to keep one all together or a straw hat to fight off the sun, but that was about all. If some fancy lace was needed for the third petticoat, a ball of crochet cotton would be purchased. Once more that was the "makins."

The hardware inventory that was required by the farmers or Uncle Billy Merchant to keep the wheels turning was also available. The stock included nails, bolts, lag screws, rivets, chain, hooks, hand tools of all kinds for the field, garden and home, leather belting, harnesses, collars, pads, fly nets, veterinary supplies, whiffletrees, eveners, clevis, neckyokes, everything for the woodsman, the carpenter, home butcher, housewife and the hired hands.

Art Carrier had a gasoline hand pump as soon as automobiles began to stir up the dust on Main Street in Duffield. Before that he had coal oil for the lantern and lamps, lubricators for the steam engines and Bag Balm for the milkmaid.

Farm machinery was available on order. He carried a stack of catalogs, on the shelf, for the farmers to wish through on their Saturday night uptown. He stocked walking plows, mowers, single row cultivators, A tooth stump drags, and good wagons. It was related that one time Art Carrier had an entire carload of knocked down new Studebaker wagons come into Duffield. For

ARTHUR CARRIER, COUNTRY MERCHANT

Arthur Carrier was the Country Merchant Extraordinaire. He looked and lived the role 100% every day.

THE MERCHANT'S WIFE

Mrs. Ova (Barker) Carrier basking in the sun on the store steps. Note Gleaner Hall in background and coal oil lamp bracketed on store front.

THE INSTITUTION, ROLLIN' ALONG

The Studebaker Wagon is sold here. Note the scales, bread box for railroad shipping, crocks, two wheel hand trucks, barrels and bags of basics. Also the Sells-Floto Circus is coming soon.

some unbeknown reason they were not acceptable. The Studebaker people would not take them back. After several days the railroad hands unloaded them and threw them in the ditch behind the depot. What ever happened to the wagons? No one seems to know.

With the closing of the Atherton Store, the post office was moved to the Carrier Store. A post office was first identified with Duffield in 1879 or two years after the railroad became operational. The post office was officially established June 13, 1884 with Charles A. Hurd appointed as Duffield's first postmaster. The office was discontinued June 30, 1927. There never was a rural mail route out of Duffield, it was a walk-in office for local patrons when postcards could be sent for a penny and a letter for three cents. This one thing insured a lot of store traffic and was good for business.

A unique feature of the Carrier General Store was the four country telephone lines. The store had lines to Durand, Gaines, Swartz Creek, and Lennon. This responsibility was both good and bad for business. Here is a true incident that my mother instigated. We had a Swartz Creek phone. She wished to talk to Boyd Cozadd, hardwareman in Gaines, who was her uncle. To save the long distance toll, of perhaps ten cents, she rang up Art Carrier in his store, whom she traded with at least once a week. How could he refuse her this small favor?

"Mr. Carrier, this is Rubena, would you please ring my Uncle Boyd at his store in Gaines."

"Sure," genial easy going Arthur would reply, "wait just a minute until I finish grinding this coffee for Hila (O'Brien)."

Art knew everybody's ring on all four lines by heart. Some rainy days he would handle more phone calls than the centrals in various towns. Those phones were all the old-fashioned wall style and there was no way the mouthpiece could be hooked up with a receiver. The messages had to be relayed verbally. This is one of the ways he earned the title of "Mr. Duffield."

In the wintertime and on rainy days the circle of hangers-on around the potbellied stove was the official "Gaines Township Forum." Discussions of politics were the rule rather than the exception. No candidate of local stature could hope to be elected unless he first was approved by the Forum in Carrier's General Store.

Market prices for produce were quoted at Art's Store and duplicated elsewhere. The Gaines phone would ring.

"Arthur, what are you paying for brown eggs today?"

"Eight cents a dozen, but they must be clean," would come back the prompt reply.

"Thank you."

That was the way it was for years and years. This store was the heartbeat of the Duffield Community until accounts on the books began to pile up. To make a long story short, he was just too nice, too easy going and he would trust anyone that needed credit—these false friends caused his fiscal failure.

COL. FENTON C. PERKINS

Fent Perkins at 19 upon his return from Auction School in Trenton, Missouri. The title of Colonel was bestowed on all young aspiring auctioneers. He dispersed the Carrier Store on order by the secured parties and was auctioneer for Dan McCaughna when John Burton suffered his fatal heart attack.

It fell upon Fenton C. Perkins, to sell the remaining inventory for the secured parties at public auction. It took three days. I remember it well because I was there, all the time, helping by handing up boxes to be sold. Inventory had been piled to the ceiling for years and a customer seldom returned home without the needed item. My father did not relish his job. He knew the Duffield Community had lost much prestige with the closing of this business.

A few other stores followed. Charles Brugger took up the Carrier Store for a few years and operated it in a reduced capacity.

Delbert and Mary Carrier had a store on the west side of the road on the second lot north of the corner with a seasonal cider mill and cement block plant.

Henry Nimphie ran a gas station on the northwest corner of Reid and Duffield Roads and there was also the famous Owls Nest that was well patronized. E. I. Brown, husband of Bernice (North Duffield teacher and baseball umpire), and father of Robert, Donna and Ardis, was the proprietor of the Owls Nest Store and euchre social club. He sold Diamond X Gasoline. His daughters were responsible for the janitorial duties, which they did not mind, except for the spittoon detail.

To the best of the writer's ability this about completes the rundown of retail merchants from information that has been made available.

At times, there was activity uptown besides the business that was transacted. Commotions on the streets of Duffield, only two with no side streets, were minimal. There was a country blade, Glen "Dick" Sage who was, it was said, as wild as a chicken hawk when he was young. He lived north of town a couple of miles and had the ability to careen a Model T about the town much to the admiration of the girls and fright of the horses tied to the hitching posts.

Feuding was non-existent, but straight street fighting was never outlawed. For instance, there was a Charlie Carpet who held out west of town and was alleged by some to be a bootlegger. There was no direct proof so nothing was ever said in public, but you know how kids are. They started hollering around town what they had heard privately in their own homes.

MARIA WARNER CARRIER

Born February 28, 1837, Died February 18, 1914. Was a daughter of Jabez and Mary Warner and the mother of Adelbert, Arthur, Alfred, Mary Carrier Scott and Lyman. The Carrier Family owned considerable acreage about Duffield.

ADELBERT CARRIER FAMILY
Adelbert Carrier and wife Lillian (Woods) with sons left to right: Lester, Claude and Delbert.

There was quite a fracas and a fist fight or two before the situation was quieted down.

The sugar beet was strong economically in the Duffield area for fifty years. It provided a cash crop for the farmers, supplementary business for the merchants and the railroad, plus it increased the population.

In the years of greatest activity, 1885 through 1925, three sugar companies had fieldmen in the vicinity. The companies were the Owosso Sugar Company, Mt. Clemens Sugar Co. and Saginaw Sugar Co. Some of the fieldmen were Frank D. Bloss, Bill Hynes, Henry Nimphie, Lloyd Thomas, Daniel Dolehanty, Bert Harris, Ernest Burleson and Joseph Dickinson.

These fieldmen would call upon farmers, within team and wagon hauling distance of the Duffield scales and beet yard, before the roads broke up in the spring. It was a competitive business. The largest and best farmers were contacted first, to try to get them to sign a contract on the dotted line to plant so many acres of sugar beets to be delivered to the scales for X dollars a ton. There was even a clause in the contract for the cook. It gave the producer the privilege of buying back sugar by the hundred pounds at cost. I can remember our family going to the railroad siding in Duffield, a bit before Christmas, with a clean wagon box padded with bright straw to pick up 500 pounds of white granulated sugar contained in cotton bags out of a red boxcar. It cost 2½ cents a pound and you did not have to pay for it. It would be deducted from your final check from the sugar company in the spring. Hank Nimphie was the fieldman. We had a skittish team, old Roxy and Don, that could not be driven, lead or pushed within twenty foot of that sugar laden boxcar. All the other people laughed at my father, Fenton. He had to carry our family supply of sugar from the car to the wagon. Then the team nearly ran away. Dad said they were scared of the white sacks.

There was some finagling in the sugar beet business. Duffield Yards was no exception. Beets were pitched on wagons from piles in the fields. If a farmer happened upon a whitish granite rock about the size of a beet he would be tempted to pitch that on the load too. When you pulled on the scales the fieldman would come out with a pail and take a sample of your beets to check the tare for dirt that would be clinging to your beets. In a wet fall the tare could be considerable. A farmer would be careful to place clean beets all around the edge of the wagon rack and the dirty ones would be piled or hid in the middle. Another bit of chiseling could be carried on by the way of a loose board in the floor of the wagon rack that would slide back and forth. As soon as the farmer forked his load of beets into an open car or on the pile he would turn his team and head back to the scales, all the time trying to get as much as possible of the loose dirt on his rack down through that loose board. It has been said, that this was one time that it was best to have a slow team.

Before the season was over the fieldman would have the chislers sorted out. Next year they would not be offered a contract.

There was another effect upon the community in addition to the economic impact. It was a social effect. Laborers were needed for field work. Eastern European families were brought in by the sugar companies, under contract, to do this work.

After planting the beets, plants were thinned to insure a uniform stand. During the summer growing season the beets were cultivated several times by the farmer and hoed twice by the field workers. There were no herbicides. At harvest the farmer lifted the beets, one row at a time, with a tool that resembled a plow without a moldboard. Hand labor was again required to go down these rows, pick up two beets at a time, beat them together to knock off the excess soil, and toss them into convenient piles. Usually six rows were combined into a row of piles. This made room for a team and wagon to be driven in between the piles when the beets were hauled to the weigh station. The final operation for the field worker was to top the beets. This was done with a beet knife that had a hook on the end for picking up beets out of this first pile. The tops were used to cover the pile of finished beets to control shrinkage and to protect them from freezing. After the beets were hauled the tops were used as cattle feed.

It was seasonal work. Some families came, they were staked by the sugar companies, provided with the essentials such as temporary housing, transported back and forth to designated

SUGAR BEETS

Sugar beets on the Clarence Ackerman Farm in about the year 1925. They contracted 100 acres a year and were the largest growers in the area at that time. Beets were the best cash crop for farmers with bottom land.

fields, paid for their labor by the acre and were never seen again. However, others who liked the community and in turn were liked by the farmers secured year round employment. Eventually, they bought homes and farms. The descendants of these sugar beet field workers are today among our most cherished neighbors, without exception.

Duffield was always noted for its Halloween pranks, like snitching Art Carrier's driving horse out of the shed behind the store and tying her to a tree in Aunt Sophie Whitmore's orchard, or moving Uncle Billy Ackerman's entire field of shocked corn from the field to the middle of the road near the North Duffield School. One of the best ones had to do with a sugar beet shanty or scale house. Jim and Bill Hynes were Irish bachelor brothers. They lived with their parents and later their spinster sister, Nellie, kept house for them. The young lads of the community seemed to come up with something special for Jim and Bill every year. They both worked in the beet business. Their beet shanty had a nice potbellied stove in it with a block chimney laid up on the outside. The Halloweeners thought they should pack the stove full of sugar beets. Why not? There were tons of them just outside the door. So they did.

They slammed the door on this stove and one of the rascals remarked, "There is room for more in the chimney."

So a couple of them scampered up on the roof of that beet scale house like a pair of red squirrels. The fellows on the ground started tossing beets to the red squirrels straddling the roof, for dropping down the chimney.

"Hey! I've a better idea, go across to Martin Drlik's and fetch us one of them small posts leaning 'agin' the back side of his pig pen."

So they did. Now, with plenty of beets and a post for a ramrod they proceeded to solidify that chimney.

When the Hynes Brothers went over to open up for business the next morning it was chilly. They were wanting to start a fire. Bill opened the stove door. A few beets rolled out on the floor, they pried a few more loose and Jim gave up in disgust.

"You know Bill, these young knuckleheads about Duffield have had their fun again and we have ended up with one constipated heating system."

POTATO DIGGER

A brand new potato digger that handled one row. It shook dirt off the potatoes and scattered them back on the ground where they had to be picked up and sorted with backbreaking effort. Note the teams. A pair of dappled greys and a span of blacks all with fly nets.

Identification of people is not definite but thought to be Frank and Elma Ackerman with children William and Katherine.

For many years, west of this beet yard, there was a stockyard owned by the railroad that was used mostly for the shipping in of feeder lambs by the Aurands, who by this time were the owners of the Frank Mapes place on Grand Blanc Road. Bert Carrier, in 1912, bought a carload of Texas Longhorns that were shipped to him and unloaded in the Duffield Stockyard. They were driven north on Duffield Road to the Carrier pasture without incident, much to the surprise of the local people.

Between the beet yard and the stockyard was a hay shed that would hold five carloads of baled hay. It was used as a storage and shipping dock by various local hay buyers such as Ford Chapman of Lennon, George Judson of Durand and Herb Frutchey of Gaines. The relating of the ability of Ford Chapman as a bale handler has been told many times by people who have witnessed his feat of strength. However, so that it will be placed in this record for posterity, it is worth repeating "one more time."

Ford Chapman owned and operated the Lennon Elevator. In the days of horses for power, hay was an important cash commodity. Ford was about 5 foot 6 inches tall, weighed two hundred thirty pounds, with shoulders like a horse and arms as strong as a young oak tree. He was a great joker and never allergic to making a wager. He was also a master at setting a trap for a salesman or some city slicker who might be on the premises. Suppose he was loading out a carload of hay by tossing up old-fashioned 100 pound bales to a couple fellows stacking them way back in the car. He would be visiting with a well dressed salesman as he worked. Ford would miss with a couple bales. They might fall down between the boxcar and the hay shed so that they had to be lifted up out of there. He would do this on purpose to bait the salesman into a substantial wager.

He might say, "I am not feeling my oats today but I'll bet you a bundle of those 2 bushel size cotton grain bags you are trying to sell me, that I can throw a bale of hay over that boxcar without touching it."

The wager would be on. Ford could do it every time. Sometimes he would take their cash. The local people loved his antics and would talk for days about how Ford took that guy to the cleaners.

Duffield had a Farmers Elevator of its own, a portion of which is still standing, but not in operating condition. It was constructed by M. G. Holmes in 1929. He bought grain, sold feed, ground grist, employed women of the area as bean pickers and ran a sawmill on the side. Noble Brothers of Flushing bought it out and the last known manager was a fellow referred to as the "Blue Line Hustler" who previously was an implement salesman. His name was Hatherill.

Agriculture was dominant in this fourth quadrant of Gaines Township. It was the foundation business. Its "root hog or die" attitude was the basic. Most landowners were thrifty general farmers. Those who were not, sold out and became day laborers. Those who had the desire to excel began to specialize with projects of their choice. These included field crops, fruit and various types of livestock.

DUFFIELD FARMERS ELEVATOR

This elevator in Genesee county located at a station stop on the Grand Trunk railway where its tracks cross the Duffield road one mile east of the Genesee-Shiawassee county line, has served as the birthplace of a new marketing program for beans. Myron R. Churchill, industrial research engineer residing at Fenton, has found time between automotive researches during the past year to put to practical test a plan to help bean growers obtain a larger share of the consumers' bean dollars. The ultimate plan provides for the establishment of a chain of such grading or processing plants throughout the bean region of Michigan under the guidance of an overall group to be known as the Michigan Bean Foundation.

THRESHING WHEAT WITH THE GREYHOUND 20 H.P.

Threshing wheat at the Frank Ackerman Farm on Hill Road with a Greyhound 20 H.P. engine that was his pride and joy. Notice the men lined up at the bagger. Grain was taken from the separator in two bushel bags (120 pounds) and carried to a granary. In this threshing the blower on the separator is not visible because it was inside the barn. The fellow who was leveling off the straw inside the barn had to have the dustiest job in the world. He would need something to cut that dust from his throat when he came down out of the mow for supper.

One of those who excelled by the way of his chosen vehicle was Augustus (Uncle Gus) Deake who was in what we now refer to as truck gardening. His residence was at 11200 West Hill Road. He owned considerable acreage of the black bottom land between the railroad and Hill Road and hired all the young people he could latch on to for weeding and harvesting. In

REO SPEEDWAGON HARNESSED TO LOAD OF HAY

The truck pulling the hay loader (a late labor saving device) was a 1923 Reo Speedwagon that has been restored to mint condition and is now used in parades and exhibited in antique shows. Frank Ackerman is on the load with fork, Edwin Millard is going to the cab, small girl is Katherine (Ackerman) Bruce, Bill Ackerman is under the large hat, and Marian (Post) Newman.

season, daily shipments were made out of Duffield via the baggage cars of the passenger trains. His best crops were onions and potatoes.

This same soil that lays all the way from Sheridan Avenue on the west to Elms Road on the east is not being utilized for its potential at this time. There has been a definite deterioration there. Some of this black, near muck soil, has even been mined. Only a waste land of brush and subsoil remains.

In yesteryear, hay, bedding and grain, for the large horse population were sources of cash income. Straight timothy hay was the most valuable commodity. Fields were rogued in the spring to insure purity of the crop. Most every farmer had surplus hay to sell. During the late winter hay buyers roamed the

RESTORED TRUCK IN PARADE FORM

The same Reo Speedwagon restored and in parade form.

vicinity like locusts in August. Hay by the carload was shipped from all the local stations, but Duffield never took the back seat to any of them.

Hay was made in June and hauled to barns or stacked loose. It had to be baled after selling and before shipping. This was usually a part of the deal with the hay buyer. Crews of men and equipment moved from farm to farm baling hay in the off-season. They were boarded by and put up for the night with whichever farm family they happened to be baling for.

Early balers, that shoved out huge bales by present standards, were powered by sweeps and tumbling rods with two or three teams attached. They would be rotated about every two hours as the horses tired. Later steam power was used and later still, the belt drive petroleum tractor was standard, before everything went modern.

BALING HAY OUT OF THE FIELD

One of the first field pickup balers in Michigan. It was pulled about the field by a tractor, derived its power from an auxiliary engine (usually balky when stalled hot) mounted on the front of the baler frame. It was a three wire hand tie and pushed out a bale weighing up to 125 pounds. The plunger was hand fed and boards were dropped manually into the bale chamber at the ring of a bell or when one of the wire pokers would holler "board." The crew, this day, was left to right: George Wilson, John E. Post, John (Jonnie) Post 3rd, Ed Post, Bill Ackerman on bale dump trailer and Curly DeBarr on the bench ready to tie the next set of wires, with his back to camera.

E. I. Brown and John Post, among others, were in this business. The records of John Post have revealed a list of men that were available for baling, general farm labor and to work in the gravel pit. Some of these were gandy dancers while others lived in the area and were stable citizens.

The list is included here as compiled by his wife Bula.

Will Tucker	Claude Carrier	Albert Hunt
Arthur Brown	Del Carrier	Walt Burgess
Dwight Burton	Emmett Brown	Bernie Burgess
Joe Ferguson	Kenneth Cole	Elton Hunter
3 Dummies	Archie Cole	Jay Hunter
Theodore Moses	Shakey Cole	Roy Ferguson
Marion Hall	Wilsey Rice	Artie O. Burns
Duffy Smith	Fred Jacobs	Harland Wickum
Earl Brunely	Ellis Humbert	Roy Wilkerson
Marshall Chaney	T. S. O'Brien	Jim Tucker
Leo Parkhurst	Clyde Woods	John Foster
Glen Sage	John Durling	Dode Kenyon
Elsworth Sage	John Haist	Ike Lyons
Lester Carrier		

The greatest revolution in agriculture came in the harvesting operation. As in baling hay, the Duffield area was progressive. The Wednesday, August 5, 1936 issue of the Flint Journal carried six photos and a news story concerning a new combine.

> Five acres of oats yielded 375 bushels of grain when harvested this week on the Perkins Farm two miles north of Duffield on Miller Road. That is sufficiently timely and important to qualify as first class farm news in these days of arid weather, but far the most important feature of this operation was that the stand of oats was harvested and threshed in one farm operation with a new combine.
>
> Outstanding among the features of this latest creation is its compactness. Only one man is required to operate it and he confines his attention largely to driving the tractor. The owner expects to use it in harvesting grain on at least fifteen Genesee County Farms this year.

This was the local beginning of the end for the large threshing outfits with crews of twenty men. This was the end of the grain binder and the shocking of grain in the field. There have been engineering improvements in this tool but the basic fact remains the same. It took away the drudgery and it was a great labor saving device.

However, something was also lost. Lost was the neighborliness that went with working together in a threshing crew around the particular area until the harvest was in the bin. The women also assisted each other in preparing the food for these large hungry crews. Everyone "traded off" with one another until the job was completed and then there was a barn dance. It was a way of life and it was good.

THREE GENERATIONS THRESH WITH NEW MACHINE

William S. Perkins in white shirt. Fenton C. Perkins on a Model G.P. Stan Perkins standing on top of new No. 6 combine. Lawrence Logie with the team and shovel. All making history with the first power take off combine on August 1, 1936.

Each steading was the virgin source of about everything that was needed to keep body and soul together except for fruits. Production took time. The cultivating and pruning went on for years before the first Greasy Pippin, Maiden Blush Apple or Russet Pear was ready for the picking. There were also more pressing things to do than to buy trees and set out an orchard on some of your best drained soil. However, at least one pioneer went counter to the trend. He was Putnam Burton, sire of the Burton family whose homestead still prevails on the northwest corner of Hill and Nichols Roads. History records his winnings at the 1851 Genesee County Fair.

Your writer is tied to that lineage through his grandmother, Henrietta (Nettie) Perkins, who was a daughter of Putnam Burton and in a founders capacity in the re-establishment of the present Genesee County Fair.

On these Duffield area farms, as far as livestock and poultry was concerned, they had it all. Much transferring and dealing of seed stock took place to eliminate inbreeding. Cattle were by far the most popular, as they are today, with horses and sheep following in that order. With the first settlers cattle were the essential. They were used as beasts of burden, for milk, meat and leather. Their manure was the only fertilizer at hand for the small winter wheat fields. Horses at first were a luxury. Sheep were a necessity because of the need for wool.

Richard, William and T. Richard Hale were prominent sheep breeders for three generations. E. C. Woods transmitted this husbandry to his son Curtis, his grandson Harry, and to great-grandson Richard. Posts and Ackermans bought western ewes by the carload. The Aurand family, who took up the Frank Mapes property on Grand Blanc Road, were volume feeders of western lambs along with a few others. They came into Duffield by the carload, weighing 50 pounds each, and were driven to the feedlots. In a few weeks they returned by the same route, fat as fools, weighing 100 pounds each, headed for the stockyard in Buffalo, New York and their reward via the same band of steel.

Horse breeding was a lucrative business. Percheron, Belgian, Clydesdale, Morgan and Hambletonian stallions cantered all the country roads showing their wares and booking probable breeding dates of mares when they were calculated to be in season.

FIRST PRIZE APPLES GENESEE COUNTY FAIR 1851

Putnam Burton with his 1st prize apples at the Genesee County Fair in 1851. Born 1829 in Seneca County, New York. Died, September 26, 1911. Father of Charles, Hamp, Dwight, Rose (Wray), Della (Harle), Henrietta (Perkins).

Payment for stud service was expected when a foal was on the ground, in good condition, and three days old. Usually they traveled more miles collecting the fees than they did delivering the service because ready cash was scarce. Records do not substantiate the stalling of breeding stallions in the immediate Duffield area but tremendous improvement was wrought by crossing these beautiful imported stallions with the native mares that were mostly western mustangs.

Of late, a scattered horse and pony population is utilized for pleasure except for one impressive establishment on a portion of the William Harris Farm. Richard C. Spike, D.V.M., and his family purchased the steading in 1969 and since have built a half mile track and become deeply involved in Standard Bred Race Horses. He does rehabilitation work on unsound horses, conditions and trains them, and has been a successful driver on Michigan tracks.

Purse $2500
GOLDENGLO at WOLVERINE RACEWAY 4/12/1982.
Owned by RICHARD and MADELON SPIKE,
Trained and Driven by RICHARD SPIKE, 1 Mile in 2:04.3, FAST.

"AND THE WIN-NAH IS, GOLDENGLO"

Dr. Richard C. Spike has a "winnah" with Goldenglo. He is holding the reins.

Governor Henry Howland Crapo, at one time, owned a quarter section the first mile north of Duffield. He was also influential in having the railroad built where it is to assist in the drainage of his bottom land and to provide a station near his main buildings. The western extremity of his holding was only one mile east of Duffield station. Even though the Crapo Farms address was that of an adjacent town and brought fame to that (now) city it must be recognized that the great herd of Hereford cattle bred there for over three generations did have an upgrading effect upon the local cattle population. Not by one of their great sires jumping the fence, but because of the favorable attitude of the likes of William "Bill" Crapo. An outstanding family of Missouri cattlemen was induced to take up residence on Crapo Farms to work with the breeding herd and to fit and show the Herefords throughout the width and breadth of this

CARLOS DOMINO 16 C.F. AND HIS KEEPERS

Carlos Domino 16th C.F. Grand Champion Hereford bull at Michigan State Fair 1940. His Honor's servants are left to right: Lee Purdy, Wayne Purdy, John Borcek and Richard Purdy beside the show barn at Crapo Farms.

land. The family name was Purdy. One branch of this family resides at Duffield headed by Wayne.

Broadblade Farms, two miles north of Duffield, established a Scotch Shorthorn herd in 1914 by W. S. and F. C. Perkins. They excelled with their products at fat stock shows. Registered livestock cattle sales were held by this firm the same as by Crapo Farms and also by a leading Holstein breeder of this area named Postdale Farms. A scion of the Perkins Shorthorn breeding family used the cattle business as a vehicle, through the route of breeding, showing and judging, to become a promotional fieldman and eventually a Purebred Livestock Auctioneer. Broadblade Farms, since the dispersal of the Shorthorns has become a steer feeding enterprise.

This firm also operated a killing floor with the Cabin Market as its retail outlet.

BROADBLADE FARM DISPERSAL AUCTION 1948

Willard Hall, Herdsman, Marshalltown, Iowa; Clinton Tomson, Secretary A.S.B.A., Wakarusa, Kansas; Jack Halsey, Auctioneer, DesMoines, Iowa.

The heifer, Broadblade Augusta, in the ring, sold to Michigan State University

A brief transition is being made here from commercial agriculture to agricultural education of youth. 4-H Clubs are sponsored by the Michigan and United States Departments of Agriculture. They have rivaled our Church Sunday School in their success in

DUFFIELD PEOPLE AT JUNIOR LIVESTOCK SHOW 1957

Duffield people at Michigan Junior Livestock Show, State Fair Grounds, Detroit in December, 1957.

Marilyn Perkins (Scheidemantel) working on her steer. She now holds a Masters Degree in Education and is a teacher at Hamady High School near Flint.

Wayne Purdy, was the 4-H Club Leader for the local livestock group and became a Genesee County 4-H Programmer. He and his wife Beth (Morrish) own the Hynes Farm in Duffield. They have five boys.

Stan Perkins, cattleman and retired 4-H Club Leader.

Spectator in plaid shirt watching Marilyn to see how it is done.

GRAND CHAMPION

Thomas Partridge and his mother June with his Grand Champion Steer at the Michigan Junior Livestock Show, State Fairgrounds, Detroit in December 1959.

This Angus steer was purchased as a calf from Meadowbrook Farms, Rochester, Michigan, now the site of Oakland University. Tom has a B.A. from Michigan State University, East Lansing.

the development of the youth of the Duffield Community. All local leadership is on a voluntary basis. Wayne Morgan has been the livestock leader for the last ten years. There are a multitude of competitive projects in which many of the local youth participate.

We were fortunate in securing a few photos of successful livestock projects that may serve as an inspiration for young people of the future.

A FAIR DAY

Maxine Perkins with a buyer representing Kroger Stores, with her 1959 Grand Champion Steer of the Michigan 4-H Show, East Lansing. She later received a degree in Mathematics from Michigan State University and took a position with Bell Labs in New Jersey where she married a scientist, George Ryva. They have two children.

Alfred Vincent, whose fine steading was less than three miles northwest of Duffield as the crow flies, on the Bennington Road, developed the top Jersey herd in America through a lifetime of study, selection and attention to fine points of breeding. When Mr. Vincent became infirm and could not care for it himself the herd was sold intact to the University of Virginia, Blacksburg, Virginia for a record price.

An outstanding registered Guernsey dairy herd was established at a showplace farm on the northwest corner of Reid and VanVleet Roads by Wray S. Boist and son Walter who was also a musician and active in the Methodist church at Duffield.

MELISSA AND KATRINA

Katrina, Champion Market Lamb of the 1975 Genesee County Fair with its owner, Melissa McLaren, member of the local 4-H Club. She is a student at Central Michigan University, Mt. Pleasant.

Jack Bancroft, a Flint trucking executive, purchased this fine farm, along with another Boist farm, one mile west of Duffield and established a registered Holstein herd. Howard Loss, a Flint undertaker, later purchased the farm east of Duffield and continued the herd until his passing.

Georgetta Farms, owned by George Behnke and later Bert Craven on the northwest corner of Grand Blanc and Duffield Roads, was a large milk production facility with a hundred cows on the line for many years.

Presently the Johnson Hackney Farm on Sheridan Avenue corner of Garrison Road is the unchallenged top milk producer of the Duffield community. His Holstein herd has earned many state awards. The only other remaining dairyman in the area is Milan Nechvil at 11207 Hill Road.

CHAMPION MARKET HOG

Champion Market Hog of the 1972 Genesee County Fair exhibited by Jeff Purdy of the local livestock club. Albert Feke of Feke & Yott was the buyer at the annual auction. Jeff has a degree in Horticulture from Michigan State University, East Lansing.

One cannot predict where the urge to excel will break out next. This was the situation on Hill Road at the Post residence when John E. decided to establish a registered Holstein herd. He made his mark in a short period in comparison to the years it took men such as Alfred Vincent to accomplish their goals. For a beginning he jumped in with both feet and purchased the entire Holstein herd of J. F. Rieman of Flint, Michigan. He soon had a cow who established a new world milk production record of that date for a 4 year old, thus bringing to Duffield nationwide recognition.

NEW WORLD'S CHAMPION PRODUCER

Lilith Segis Inka de Kol Johan 616923. New World's Champion Junior 4-year-old for milk production. 862.6 lbs. milk, 29.23 lbs. butter, in 7 days; 3435 lbs. milk, 115.27 lbs. butter in 30 days. (Figures from official tester.) Owned by John E. Post, Duffield, Mich.

Take the road out of Duffield to Postdale Farms, and you'll find a stable full of mighty nice Holstein cows. They are of good size, in excellent condition, and have the strong loins, broad hips, deep bodies, and capacious udders that mark the milk and money cow.

The owner of the farms and herd is John E. Post, a man who is young enough to be enthusiastic and old enough to realize that to do worthwhile work requires a purebred herd and careful handling.

After looking over the herd, we wanted to know how he came to have such an evenly excellent lot. There are not many herds of the size of the Postdale lot, forty-seven head, which show such uniformity of size and type and dairy quality, either in Michigan or any other state.

Said Mr. Post, "Two years ago, I didn't have a single purebred; but I made up my mind that there was no use fooling around with grades, and I bought a few head from J. E. Rieman, of Flint. Later on I bought the rest of them, thirty-four head in all, and most of the herd are of his line of breeding."

There has been $3,500 worth of stock sold off the farm and there still are forty-seven head of Holsteins left.

Besides feeding 120 lbs. a day to calves, Postdale Farms trucks 12 cans or 1,032 lbs. milk a day into Flint. The price of milk on the day this was written, the last week in March was $2.45 per cwt. net, and Mr. Post wasn't crepe hanging over it, in welcome contrast to the general run of dairy farmer

From Holstein-Friesian World
May 10, 1924

John Post became enthused to the extent that he traveled to Massachusetts and purchased a particular herd bull prospect at a previously unheard of high figure to do some selective breeding. A combination of situations caused his ardor to cool. After only a few years the Postdale Herd was dispersed on November 14, 1924.

The largest volume business in the Duffield area was John Post and Sons Aggregate Supply and its subsidiary the Transit Mix Company. The plant was at 6017 Sheridan Avenue. It is now a pit-side housing development.

Early maps of section 7 Gaines Township revealed unusual physical characteristics. There were mineral springs, muck, clay

AERIAL VIEW OF POST & SONS PIT IN OPERATION

Air view of John Post and Sons Aggregate Supply Company. The road in the foreground is Sheridan Avenue.

VALLEY FARM EQUIPMENT

A new business on Grand Blanc Road opened in 1982 and owned by Frank Farro and Son.

with ferrous oxide and gravel. After much dabbling in the deposit for three generations, as necessity required, John E. Post took up the challenge and opened a pit in the spring of 1947 with modern machinery. Three sons provided excellent support and over a period of 19 years over a million yards of aggregate were mined and processed at this location. It added much to the local economy.

Not since Art Carrier's General Store sold Studebaker wagons and other horse powered farm tools has there been a farm implement business about Duffield.

This spring of 1982 Valley Farm Equipment opened for business at 11309 Grand Blanc Road on a portion of the old M. Halpin acreage. It is an Allis-Chalmers dealership. An efficient modern steel building has been constructed and the grounds have been landscaped. Frank Farro and son Steve are the owners.

Michael Welch was a cantankerous son of Erin who at one time held title to 60 acres two miles north of Duffield in section 31 of Clayton Township. He was involved in several litigations over line fence, drainage, etc. with his neighbors and finally found himself between a sharp rock and a hard place because of his inability to pay the lawyers fees. He lost the property and it was

ASPLIN CIDER MILL

The Asplin Cider Mill located on Miller Road—a busy place in season. A sample of Christmas trees that are merchandised from Thanksgiving on are in the foreground.

eventually purchased by a Rev. Glen R. Asplin. The property backed up to Sandhill Bill Shaw's place and the soil was about the same quality. Being as how the Rev. Glen was a do-gooder, he planted the Welch Farm to fruit and pine trees.

The property has passed on to a son, Wendell G., who has taken advantage of his father's soil conservation practices. Present activities, in season, include a cider mill, Christmas tree sales, a Bluegrass Festival and other recreational events that are a credit to the Duffield Community.

CHAPTER IX

THE HUMAN SIDE

DUFFIELD WAS NON-EXISTENT as a town before the coming of the railroad in 1877. It has nearly returned to its original status since the station was closed in 1931. Thus, the circle has been completed. Previously the story of the jockeying for position by financiers and the actual construction of the ribbon of steel has been told. The reiteration of the human side, in connection with the railroad, remains. As far as the Duffield Community is concerned the human side is of equal importance. This facet is twofold. First, it has to do with the generation of local business and second, the personal effect on local people in their public and private lives. These human situations cover the entire spectrum of local life from the humorous to the tragic.

Roads about the countryside at several seasons of the year were nye impassable, but the trains were available and on time.

There were two local freights each day except Sunday. One would start from Port Huron and go west to Durand. That was a days run. Hotels, owned by the railroad, were available for the crews at each end of the line. The other local freight would travel in the opposite direction. At one time four passenger trains stopped at the Duffield Station every twenty-four hours, seven days a week. The odd numbered trains went west. The even numbered ones went east.

According to Sylvester Holman "Mac" Maginity, railroad engineer, there were only a few times that the trains did not roll

THE LIFELINE

The lifeline of many midwestern towns and villages was the railroad. It made them the focal point for transportation, mail, freight, and related business. When this need decreased because of other trade channels the towns and villages wilted as did Duffield, Michigan.

through Duffield. During the winter of 1916 a great snowstorm shut the trains down and another time several carloads of iced dressed beef tore up both tracks forty rods west of the county line. With a double track usually one would remain operative.

Some of the most valuable trains that passed through Duffield were the Silk Trains enroute to the New York garment industry. Mac would be the engineer on the Pilot Train that preceded the Silk Trains to check the track.

During World War I, within 24 hours, troop trains started a whole division of Doughboys from Camp Custer on the first leg of their journey to the European Western Front. These were the most precious trains. Jess Hardick, son of LeGrand Hardick, and Glen Harle, son of George Harle, were enroute on these trains. Jess was killed in Germany. Glen returned to his family whose farm was next to the Doane School. Clement and James Hynes also returned home safe and sound.

Railroads were beneficial, but gross progress always has its minor drawbacks. As soon as a railroad became operable adjacent land prices were inflated at the rate of $10.00 per acre with the customary jump in valuations and, of course, taxes. Livestock

TRAVELING SALESMAN AND TEAM

George Harle and son Glen, the W.W.I doughboy, all set to hit the road with a fast team and shiny weatherproof sales wagon for J. R. Watkins. He was married to one of Putnam Burton's three daughters, Della, and lived next to the Doane School.

was always breaking out and getting on the railroad tracks and being killed, especially at night. Railroads were slow to settle claims and only at 50% of the actual value. Fires along the right-of-way, caused by the engines, were yet another source of contention. Fires also happened in the boxcars and coaches because of coal oil lamps for lighting and potbellied stoves used for heat. Cars were made of wood and were an invitation to disaster. In case of a train wreck passengers were speared by the dry splinters. All of these things, in connection with the railroad took place around Duffield.

The crossing at Duffield Road was not known for its fatalities but there was one accident on the tracks that shook up the entire community. William R. Atherton had a son, Addison, who at the age of 5 years was riding on the front of a wagon with his father who was tending to the reins of a spirited team with both hands. The rough crossing of the tracks with the steel wheeled wagon shook the lad so that he fell off the wagon rack in behind the horses and in front of the wheels, and was run over and killed.

At another time a hired hand for an Irish family, south of town, was crossing the tracks with a load of loose hay and did not see an approaching freight. All was lost with a part of the wagon and a considerable amount of the hay being carried as far east as the Robert Herrick property on the cowcatcher of the engine.

The McNinney family lived in a small house on the north side of Reid Road west of town near the tracks. It has been mentioned that the father, James McNinney, lost his leg in the Spanish American War of '98. This could not be authenticated so his name was not included in the list of War Veterans. He was a hero of sorts to all the young boys because of his fancy peg leg with a wide brass band at the top to hold his stump. He was also a hero in the eyes of the Grand Trunk Railway.

The railroad trestle over Jones Creek to the southwest of his house got on fire. He extinguished the flames with water from the creek, mounted the steep roadbed, went down the track and flagged down an approaching train. He had a son Orson, who in consideration of his father's alertness, was given a position with the railroad.

Delbert "Del" Carrier, father of Delloise and Bert Carrier, had a close call with his Model T truck at the Duffield crossing. He was also hauling loose hay. It was draped out over the cab obscuring his vision. He heard a close train whistle as he approached the tracks. The wheels (to hear Del tell it) in his head began to turn about the speed of the ones on the freight train. The brakes on his truck were non-existent. Being no gambler he decided not to try and beat it, so he decided to join it. He turned off the road sharp to the right and ended up parallel to those bands of steel a wee bit too close as the mile-a-minute monster bellowed by. It nearly unloaded the hay with one swish and caught the leading edge of the left front fender of that Model T. The truck was so close to the tracks that each car in that train, as it went passing by, issued its own personal warning of clickety-clack, clickety-clack, clickety-clack by taking on that now floppy left front fender. Del sat in the flimsy cab, petrified with fear, not daring to move, until all had passed. Some witnesses to the contingency rushed over to his truck, opened the door and pulled him out, very blanched, but safe and sound.

Del was one of the great story tellers of Duffield. His embellishments of known events were masterpieces, especially when he was fishing.

The great snow of 1916 that closed down the railroad had repercussions among individuals as well. For a couple of years previous to this storm two single men had lived in a wagon house at the old Gilbert Gravel Pit (Crapo Pit). Each of them had a good span of horses with which they hired out to farmers and road builders in the summer and worked in the lumber woods during the winter. Via the railroad tracks they were less than two miles from Duffield. One came on foot up the tracks for provisions and mail with this historic 1916 northeaster at his back. It was suggested that he not attempt to return in the face of the howling sub-zero blizzard, but he could not be deterred. His body was found in the spring. No one living can recall his name, though several recall the tragedy.

Another body was found beside the tracks about eighty rods west of the county line on March 30, 1921. It was a body that was to test the ability of the Duffield Community to survive as a close-knit community. It was what remained of Lucy Wittum who was

19 years old at the time. The engineer of the eastbound No. 6 passenger train spotted ahead what appeared to be a dark bundle on the south grade about nine feet from the tracks. He had already cut the throttle for Duffield so he leaned out of the cab for a better look as he went by—by jove! there were arms and legs. He tripped the emergency brake. The train came to a screeching halt a bit west of the county line crossing.

The crew and most of the passengers piled out and ran back up the tracks to the corpse. It was a beautiful young woman. She had not been hit by a train. The trainmen picked her up and moved her further from the tracks up on the south bank. This they should not have done. Valuable evidence could have been destroyed.

Wray Boist, whose steading was at the end of Reid Road and was spread out along the north side of the tracks, west of the county line, was finishing the morning milking when he heard the commotion. He looked out the cowshed door, grabbed son Walter by the arm and over the barnyard fence they went to see what in the world was going on. Wray Boist was an important witness in both the hearing and trial that was to follow.

Authorities were summoned including Deputy Sheriff J. A. Fries and Dr. Robert C. Fair. The train and passengers were allowed to proceed after identifications were recorded, particularly of those who had moved the body.

Within thirty-six hours, following an autopsy, these facts were firmly established. Lucy Wittum's death was caused by the ingestion of (C_6H_6O) carbolic acid and she had been in "the family way" approximately sixty days. In addition her stomach was practically destroyed and there were acid burns on her arm and face. She clutched a small bottle that had contained the acid in her left hand. It was estimated that she died between midnight and two A.M. of March 30, 1921.

By this time the conservative and ofttimes sedate Duffield Community had lashed itself into a frenzy. A swarm of inquisitive newspaper reporters descended upon the area seeking additional bits of information to add to the established facts. This fueled the condition. The unanswered question was: suicide or murder?

On Saturday, April 16, 1921 a preliminary examination was held by Justice of Peace Samuel C. Patchel of Vernon Township and a decision was rendered, after the taking of considerable testimony, to bind over to Circuit Court of Shiawassee County one Forrest Higgins on the charge of murder. He was promptly arrested and held without bail in the Shiawassee County Jail, Corunna, Michigan. Forrest Higgins was divorced from his wife and lived with his parents, Mr. and Mrs. William Higgins, on the first farm south of the railroad on the west side of the county line road (Sheridan Avenue). There was in the family an infant daughter by this previous marriage.

Lucy Wittum lived across the road with her parents Asa and Jessie Wittum and two sisters, Ruth and Erma, but much closer to the tracks. The steading no longer exists. It was said that Lucy was a sociable girl who often stayed in Flint with friends and was a regular visitor and spent much time in the Burns Home that is located in the northeast corner of this intersection and now owned by Frank and Elsie Kerr. She was a close friend of the Burns boys, Arthur and Charles. Another local gentleman whose reputation was above suspicion but had the misfortune of being away from home that evening, on a late social visit, was questioned meticulously. However, it all condensed down to the individual who admitted to having been in Miss Wittum's company the night of her death. As the record implies, her travels to and from the Carrier General Store via the railroad were not always alone and not without interruptions.

The trial of Forrest Higgins began on June 21, 1921. It was presided over by Judge Joseph H. Collins. The prosecuting attorney, Roy D. Matthews, was excused because of having previously been retained in private practice by William Higgins, father of the defendant. Byron P. Hicks was engaged by the court as a special prosecutor to try the case. The attorneys for the defense were Seth Q. Pulver and A. L. Chandler of Owosso.

The jury consisted of twelve men: Charles Herman, Henry VanDeusen, John Castee, William Eddingon, Fred Sanders, William Cornwell, Joseph Augustine, Charles Drumm, George Onstot, Fred Sarver, Herman Hoover and A. J. Parkhurst. They were placed in the charge of deputies E. J. Herrick and Charles

Owen for the duration of the trial. Providing food and lodging and the censoring of all reading materials pertaining to the case were their duties. The jury was sworn in Saturday, June 25th.

Witnesses called and subpoenaed were: Daniel Gustin, Arthur Carrier, Elsie Needham, Mable Burleson, Wray and Walter Boist, Clarence Mapes, Samuel Patchel, Glen Sage, H. G. Nimphie Jr., Mable Merchant, Jim Hines, Roy Gray, Arthur Gray, Laura Crane, Godfrey Hartman, Ruth Vassar, Erma Wittum, William Higgins, Dr. James Rowley, Roy Lennon, Dr. J. A. Fries, Louis Pardee, Joseph Sproule, Bruce Robinson, J. I. Thomaszski, J. M. Cronk, F. T. Richards, H. J. Barton, Asa and Jessie Wittum, Dr. Walter Parker, Jim Dingwall, Floyd Derham, M. D. Corey, J. Downing, Harry Sheffield, A. N. Brock, Frank Hutchinson, William McMullen, W. C. Geaghley, John Barnes, Jim Bailey, Tim Riley, J. H. Sayre, R. D. Jones, M. E. Althaus, William H. Sage. In addition, one Joseph Sheridan of the State Constabulary was confined in the same cell with the defendant after April 16th for several days and claimed to have obtained a confession. However, his testimony was stricken from the record and ruled not admissible as evidence on a point of law by Judge Collins. This was before the day of the tape recorders.

It was the State of Michigan vs. Forrest Higgins, case number 1099. The charge was "that one Forrest Higgins feloniously, willfully and of his malice afterthought, did kill and murder one Lucy Wittum." The Special Prosecutor Hicks had to build his case on circumstantial evidence because there was no direct evidence that Lucy Wittum did not commit suicide. The parade of witnesses continued for several days and it boiled down to this quote taken from the records. It was "whether Lucy Wittum voluntarily and without his (the defendant's) request or knowledge and without his being able to prevent it, took carbolic acid with the intent to end her life."

Judge Collins charged the jury July 16 and after serious deliberation on July 18 they returned to the courtroom and announced that they had reached a verdict. The foreman announced with firmness, "not guilty as charged."

During the trial of Forrest Higgins, residents of the area attended the proceedings en masse. The trial lasted almost four

THE HUMAN SIDE 121

weeks. Rash conversation for conviction ran rampant with some harboring the preconceived idea of taking the law into their own hands. A solid deterrent was that the defendant was denied bail. This served three purposes. The Court was certain that Higgins would be available for trial when called. He would be under protective custody safe from the hotheads, the county had had a lynching a few years previous, and it gave the Prosecutor an opportunity to plant a stool pigeon within the same cell. A confidential confession was said to have been secured as previously mentioned. Cooler heads prevailed.

The Judge's instruction to the jury was explicit when he said, "You cannot convict on circumstantial evidence."

And so it was. It was necessary for many to do an "about face" and revert to "as you were" of military parlance. The entire episode was a severe shock to the Duffield Community. It could be compared to shock often suffered by an individual following a serious injury—but, in this instance, the patient survived, because of the forgiving attitude and understanding of its people.

As the miscellaneous events were being cataloged this thank you card came to light.

Swartz Creek, Mich.
Mar. 21, 1920

We wish to thank the Ladies Aid Society for the beautiful flowers with which they showed their sympathy in our recent bereavement.

Mrs. John Burton and Children

The passing of John Burton, son of Hampton by Putnam Burton, was a shock from which the community did not soon recover.

It was in early March, 1920. He was at an auction sale being cried by Fent Perkins at the second steading east of the corner of Reid and Nichols Roads owned by Dan McCaughna. John Burton was standing beside William Harris, longtime Gaines Township Supervisor, bidding on some geese when suddenly he

JOHN & RUTH BURTON ON THEIR WEDDING DAY

The wedding photo of John and Ruth (Colbrath) Burton. It has been said that "no finer man ever made tracks about Duffield than John Burton." They were the parents of William and Helen.

pitched forward and fell at the auctioneer's feet. It was a heart attack. He was twenty-nine years old. He left a young wife, Ruth, and two small children, William and Helen. Ruth never remarried.

In contrast, there is the death of a beautiful three year old daughter of Mr. and Mrs. Paul Drlik on September 13, 1919. At the time they lived in a small house that followed the blacksmith shop and preceded the grain elevator on the same location. It was a Sunday afternoon and little Emily somehow came upon a box of matches that she played with until her clothing was ignited. Little girls clothing at the time was voluminous. The burns were fatal.

Funds provided to the Duffield Methodist Church from the Paul Drlik Estate were used to construct and install the spire and belfry as per photo on page 34.

Some of the bottom land north of Duffield was a muskrat swamp before it was drained. Many men trapped to supplement their incomes. None were as successful as the team of Henry Nimphie and Benjamin Hillaker. They were known as Hank and Ben. They were both well liked and welcome wherever they staked a trap. A prime black skunk pelt would fetch six dollars which was more than a good farm hand, at the same time, could receive for a week's wages.

Summer mosquitoes and other health problems made it imperative that the Carrier Swamp be drained and William Thatcher was the low bidder to excavate what is known as Webb Drain. A cofferdam was built on the east side of Duffield Road to hold back the flood water from the Martin Drlik farm and other property to the east with Nichols Road as the breaking watershed line.

A floating dredge was assembled right at the point of beginning, which was the west side of Duffield Road one half mile north of town. It was steam powered.

BEN HILLAKER AND BROTHER

Benjamin Hillaker on the right, the trapper, hunter and community handyman of a past generation, with his brother, leaning on the running board of a Model T Ford Sedan.

MRS. MINA HILLAKER AND DAUGHTER

Mrs. Ben Hillaker, with daughter Pearl (wife of Rufus Gilbert whose children Elaine, Wayne, Winona, Mildred, Georgia, Arlene, Frederick and Grace went to school and church in Duffield) in the buggy hitched to an excellent driving mare named Nellie in the yard of their home on Maple Avenue (Miller Road)

Enough water was allowed to escape the dam to float the apparatus once the initial hole was completed. It was a large project and proceeded for miles until hooked into the Shiawassee River in section 31 of Venice Township of Shiawassee County. It was a great feat of engineering for that day, accrued many benefits to the public health, provided excellent drainage for thousands of acres of rich bottom land and it all began in Duffield.

There was only one difficulty that was not conquered: how to keep a supply of coal aboard to run the boiler. It was said that it took more men, horses, floats and "what have you" to get the fuel to the dredge down through the swamp, than it did to dig the ditch.

CHAPTER X

PERSONALITIES AT LARGE

THOSE FOUNDING FAMILIES who held, shall we say, franchises in the community plus the recent more mobile inhabitants were conformists. Few stuck out like sore thumbs or stubbed toes. As far as we have been able to ascertain, nary a genius protruded. The preponderance was of the run-of-the-mill law abiding citizenry.

This is the reason that in the prologue we classified the Duffield Community as a "typical mid-American area based on an agricultural economy." It is most certainly an unglorified example of a pillar of our nation as multiplied thousands of times across our land.

There was an absence of genuises around Duffield but yet many people excelled in their chosen positions of life. There were students, teachers, craftsmen and those who sought to improve. There were those who assumed responsibility and those who delegated authority. We will attempt to recognize some of these individuals at random.

Lyman Carrier was the youngest son of George Carrier who came to a goodly portion of section 7 of Gaines Township from New York State. He was a Civil War veteran and because of wartime acquired disabilities, died young and left a strong, determined widow, Maria, to raise their five children.

Lyman secured a degree in agriculture at Michigan State College in 1902. He became a professor of agriculture and a respected writer on agricultural subjects in his adopted state of Virginia. One of his contributions to literature was "Agriculture in Virginia 1607-1699." It was published in 1957 as a part of the 350th anniversary celebration of the State of Virginia. He has made his mark.

Willard Harris, son of William Harris, who was himself a Gaines Township Supervisor for 10 years, made a correct decision when he asked one Alice Mitchell to marry him. They reside on Reid Road and have one son James. They have devoted their middle and matured years to public service. Willard followed his father as supervisor for 12 years, became a county commissioner and upon retirement the commission chambers of the Genesee County Administration Building was named the Willard B. Harris Auditorium. A great honor has been bestowed on a lifetime Duffield resident.

Daniel Brown, always referred to as Uncle Daniel, was the father of Harriet Post, wife of Edward. He was a cousin to Robert Brown and grandsire of all the Posts and Ackermans. He was a man who exercised leadership at a time it was sorely needed in the educational and religious areas. He drove the best horses, maintained the finest home and never shirked duties that would be beneficial to his neighbors.

June (Perkins) Kanaar, artist and teacher of china and portrait painting, has resided on the fringe of the Duffield Community all her life. This talent which was inherited from her mother Rubena (Cozadd) Perkins has enabled her to become recognized nationwide.

Howard C. Atherton, who stubbed his toe about old Duffield as a boy, went into the Buick Factory as a common laborer and through education and experience returned as general foreman of Plant 31 of the Buick Motor Division of General Motors.

Harold L. Post, graduate of Michigan State University, manager of the family aggregate business, Chairman of the Genesee County Republican Party, owner with his wife Beverly (Swalla) of Post & Company Realtors, Flint, has recently been appointed by Governor Milliken to the Michigan Board of Realtors. Harold has always been a distinct plus to the community. He deserves all the credits listed.

You could logically state that John E. Post was the entrepreneur of Duffield. He handled all the standard activities of a normal life in stride such as marrying into the Middlesworth clan, raising three boys and a fine daughter. He maintained a good home, was an ample provider, and was honest and well liked—but he always was looking over the fence for something additional.

What jammed home this thought was the uncovering of the flyer, "Farm Gate opens from either end" shown on page 128. "I. C. Duell & Post, Manufacturers" at the bottom reveals yet another project of our beloved Johnny. He was also an innovator. Back in section 7 on the Daniel Brown Farm that John and Bula purchased for their home, they prospected for gold and found it in flake form. Geologists stated that it had been transported by glaciers of the ice age to its destination near Duffield.

According to a feature story published in the Flint Journal, June 17, 1944 and written by John Conde, John Post built a gold smelter for one Frank W. Lord of 2008 Church Street, Flint. It could be said that he was a local prospector as well as being interested in the refining process of gold.

John wildcatted for oil with the help of his boys and found it in that same section of Gaines Township. Some say that an oil well would be back there pumping the black gold today if inexperience had not caused the rupture of their casing. A large flow of heavy mineralized water soon took control. The Department of Natural Resources regulations required the well to be filled and sealed. So—there went Duffield's first oil well. It was flooded out by one of Dr. Duffield's mineral springs.

No one seems to know which came first the chicken or the egg, the gold or the oil, but the mention of either one of these spectacular discoveries was enough to keep the people up and down the roads babbling for weeks. About the time the talk quieted down someone would bring it up again or John would embark upon another project.

John E. Post's venture into the dairy cattle business was nothing less than spectacular. Within a short period of time he

FARM GATE
Opens from Either End

THIS gate has a steel frame so constructed as to be put together at the ends with interlocking sleeves so as to do away with all welded or threaded joints.

It hangs in the center on a U-shaped crane which eliminates all chances of sagging or distortion due to eccentric weight or weight bearing thereon. This feature also allows for the opening of gate from either end where it is securely fastened with a positive stop latch.

The gate can be raised or lowered up to 16 inches from the ground allowing the gate to swing free and clear after an ordinary snow fall, also to allow small animals to pass under the gate and to still retain larger animals in the field.

The materials used in this gate are so constructed as to give greater strength and satisfaction.

Patented 24th day of July 1923. Patent No. 1462766

This gate sells, according to size, for only **$9.95 up**

Be sure and place your order now for fall or spring delivery before a raise in raw materials which would automatically raise the price of the gate.

I. C. DUELL & POST
MANUFACTURERS

had, at Postdale Farm, a world record producing cow. She was from the herd of Bert Potter, a nearby dairy farmer who had never raised high producers.

Next came a headline in The Flint Journal that read, "Post Buys $5000 Bull to Aid An Already Famous Herd of Holsteins." You can only imagine the reverberations this set off among the natives. As if that was not enough activity, on the way returning from Massachusetts through Ontario, they were involved in an automobile accident that totaled out the new Buick that had been purchased especially for the trip. In the group were also John E. Post's father Edward Post, Bert Potter, John Long, and J. H. Soule. No one was injured.

John was adept at operating a sawmill and a threshing rig and initialed field pickup baling.

John attended General Motors Institute, was a member of the Chevrolet Employees Association and was one of the original contract haulers of F. J. Boutell Automobile Driveaway Company with a signing date of December 12, 1934. He was a Royal Arch Mason and always looked to for advice and leadership. His life-style and its very diversified activities were sometimes questioned by the conservative neighbors but he was Duffield's most progressive citizen for several decades.

Terrence Hynes had a son Joseph who was raised in Duffield. Joseph acquired a degree in pharmacy. At one time he owned and managed a chain of nine drugstores within the City of Detroit. A brother James also a pharmacist, had a single drugstore in Detroit during the same years and worked closely with Joseph. Taking into consideration the population of that city at the time, these two "We're From Duffield" brothers must have had things about sewed up as far as drugstores were concerned.

John and Catherine (Drlik) Nemecek, likewise raised two sons in downtown Duffield. They have made impressive records with the area's largest employer. Donald is a foreman at General

---

DUELL & POST AND THEIR FARM GATE
Bottom picture taken in 1930 at State Fairgrounds in Detroit

Motors Parts Division and Jerry H. is general foreman of the Chevrolet Die Room.

If there ever was a first family of Duffield it would have to be the John J. Middlesworth Family. There were three girls, Bula, Evlyn and Merle, that have been previously mentioned. The three boys were John J., Jr., called J.J., Ray and George. They were a musical family and could always be depended on for entertainment at social events.

J.J. was a professional with the violin, cello and piano. He traveled with the Arthur Godfrey show as a member of the band. He taught public school music and had a private studio in Clawson, Michigan at which he tutored selected students.

Ray was a veteran of World War II. He married a Mormon girl and moved west. His health was never the best.

George cast his lot with the Checker Cab Company in Kalamazoo. He began as a driver delivering new taxis and advanced to a position of drive-a-way crew foreman. One position led to another and he retired as a vice-president after having been general superintendent of a Checker Plant in Portland, Maine.

Incidently, this company ceased all manufacturing operations on July 9, 1982 in Kalamazoo.

Every city, village or hamlet has to have a mayor, official or unofficial. In Duffield it has always been unofficial. With the demise of Uncle Billy Merchant the mantle has fallen on John Drlik, son of Martin Drlik. Martin cast his lot with the community in 1910. He came by rail car with all his earthly belongings and a small family. A younger brother Paul soon followed.

The present "mayor," John Drlik and Beth (Haist) Drlik had three children and among them is John Martin Drlik, M.D., a psychiatrist. He also has a mechanical engineering degree from the University of Michigan.

Their daughter Jane (Drlik) Griesa is a teacher with a B.A. from Sacramento Teachers College, Sacramento, California and an M.A. from Rider College, Trenton, New Jersey.

Son Leslie is a local businessman and rural mail carrier.

Wayne J. Newman, son of Wayne and Marian (Post) Newman, has a Masters Degree from Central Michigan University, Mt. Pleasant and is a coach and teacher in the high school in Beal City, Michigan.

DUFFIELD HILLBILLY BAND

Bluegrass grew from the Gaines Township soil before the first settlers arrived. Bluegrass music was played in Duffield 50 years before it was in Nashville, Tennessee. In this photo, taken against Floyd Ackerman's barn door, are left to right: Floyd Ackerman, Dick Richards, Evlyn Middlesworth Ackerman, Marguerite Stevens Ackerman and Bill Ackerman. They provided the music for square dances, house parties, barn raisings, chivarees and the likes. Sometimes they just played for their own enjoyment. This is the quality that brings them to our attention.

Terrence L. Newman, a brother of Wayne J., lives a short distance away from Duffield. He is a professional musician. His major instrument is the string bass. Myron Floren of the Welk Band fame uses Terrence's talent for his personal traveling band.

He is a member of the Treasure Island Trio and the University of Michigan People's Band. His suit is jazz.

Michael L. McLaren, earned a degree in mathematics at the University of Michigan and a degree in music from Oakland University. He is band director and teacher at Grand Blanc High School and was a member of the great University of Michigan Rose Bowl Bands.

In this chapter on "Personalities at Large" the author has taken the liberty to skip about as various contributors presented material. So it goes with the illustration on the following page. This was a significant event.

Five cousins, three of whom were brothers, received their Master Mason degrees as North Newburg Lodge No. 161 F & A M met Saturday evening, April 24, 1954. About 100 persons attended from Flint, Swartz Creek, Ovid, Chesaning, Vernon, Corunna, Bancroft, Lansing and Perry.

At least six doctors live in or have been closely associated with the Duffield Community. They are:

Dr. John M. Drlik, M.D., who is a one hundred percent Duffield product. He secured his degree from the University of Michigan and is practicing in Fremont, California. His wife's name is Cynthia and they have three children. This is a perfect example of the title of this book. "We're from Duffield."

Dr. William Gensel, O.D., first studied to become a veterinarian but later in life became an optometrist with an office in Flint. He owned and made his home on the property that is now known as the James Harris Family Place. He was a pleasant soft spoken man who took part in local activities and was particularly devoted to the church.

Dr. Judith Moore, D.O., a graduate of Michigan State University, East Lansing, Michigan, has her office in the Swartz Creek Plaza where she enjoys a fine practice. Her home is a credit to Hill Road and located on a portion of the old Deake Farm.

Dr. Daniel O'Brien, M.D., was a son of Michael O'Brien. He graduated from the Detroit College of Medicine and practiced as a family doctor in Lapeer, Michigan for forty years. He was a very humorous man and was known far and wide. His roots were deep in Duffield's Little Corktown.

RECEIVING MASONIC DEGREES

Carl Post is shown receiving his Masonic apron from Ray Turner, worshipful master of North Newburg Lodge No. 161, F&AM, in ceremonies in which five cousins, three of whom are brothers, received their third degrees Saturday. Others honored were, top row, from left, Harold and Edgar Post, and John Post Jr., bottom right, and William Ackerman.—Photo Courtesy Argus-Press.

Dr. Wayne M. Raver, D.C., holds a degree from the National College of Chiropractics, Chicago, Illinois, and practices in Flint. He is a devout man of many talents. Duffield appreciates his musical ability. Dr. Wayne and his wife Onva are active in the church.

Dr. Richard C. Spike, D.V.M., has his large animal clinic, training track and home at the former William Harris property on Hill Road near Nichols Road. He earned his degree at Michigan State University, East Lansing. He is mentioned elsewhere in this publication for his achievements.

Residing on Grand Blanc Road near the site of the Halpin School is Henry "Hank" Robison who is a poet and lyricist. He has honored the Duffield Community by winning several national awards.

He was a quarter finalist award winner in the American Song Festival at Los Angeles in 1978. Also, he garnered awards from the Music City Song Festival at Nashville in 1980 both in Country and Gospel.

Hank has a very responsive talent. Thirty minutes after your writer had recounted an episode, spawned by prohibition, that had taken place in Duffield, he bobbed back in the office with the following poem.

THE DUFFIELD FLU

'Twas the good folk from Ireland
That settled in Duffield ye know.
They gave the devil his just due,
With the spirit of the Lord in their heart
And some in their belly for dust and the flu.

Come prohibition, the government said no,
And shut off the flow of usquebaugh
For some of those poor souls.
There-a-bout worked a man of devious doubt,
Who said he knew where to get this wonder brew.

They made up a kitty of twenty dollars or so,
Put him on the east bound and said, "Go-man-go."
—And he did—
They stood by the track red eyed and in pain,
Two nights and three days they waited in vain.

Their thirst got worse, their throats got hoarse,
They held a q.t. meeting and approached a new source.
Customs never search a conductor ye know,
From Canada to Duffield the water of life flowed.

Come the end of prohibition;
    Ain't too sure of the Duffield flu.

               uncle hank robison
                  the country poet

The background of information that inspired this poem was a carry-over from an informal get-together held in Uncle Billy Merchant's Blacksmith Shop. The soldiers had returned from World War I and it was the spring of 1919.

It was instigated by the men from Little Corktown with encouragement from most all the other males in the community. The subject was good whisky. During the winter some of them had run off a batch of mash and the resulting product had made them quite sick. The preacher and some of the women folk thought they had come down with the second go around of that wartime flu, but that was not so. They were not going to make home brew again, but the situation remained the same. They had to have some good quality whisky for medicine, to cut the dust they acquired during farm field work and threshing plus a nip occasionally for a Saturday night.

The fly in the ointment was prohibition. It became the law of the land January 16, 1920. For a few years previous the area had been going dry in fits and squirts overtaking townships and villages alike. However, one could get on the passenger train and go into a nearby area and buy what spirits were needed. Now, the Eighteenth Amendment had choked off that supply—so the meeting. A hired hand who knew his way around and was quite talkative volunteered to supply the need. They passed the hat and raised over $20.00 and put him on the morning train for Ontario. He was to return as soon as possible with an ample supply of good whisky which was readily available there.

Some figured he would be back the next day but he did not get off the train in Duffield. Two days and it was a no-show. The third day a group met the two westbound passenger trains that stopped at the Duffield Depot and to their disappointment he was not on either one. A week passed and they gave up. They had been taken. It has been said that some of the oldsters still have their shillelaghs at the ready should he ever return.

They tried to keep it quiet. This was impossible in a small town. The dilemma came to the attention of the depot agent. In anticipation of their needs he had a system all set up with the conductor on the Number 7 passenger train before being approached by the men of Little Corktown. Needless to say, they were pleased with the arrangement. The conductor would acquire the required spirits during his layover at customs. As a courtesy of the road his personal bags were never examined. This arrangement was used for many years without interruption or embarrassment of any description even though the principals involved changed.

None of the imported whisky was ever sold to third parties. No one ever became an alcoholic as a result. Most of it was used for its medicinal qualities. This also explains the reason why there was often an adult male waiting at the station just to watch the passenger train come in.

There has been a rumor circulating about the community for generations, that Duffield's own poet has condensed into this following verse.

ODE TO THE OPERA

Four times a day east or west
They could board a train
In their Sunday best.
Into Flint city from Duffield they'd go,
The boys and girls to the opera show.

The boys would turn their watches back,
The girls would pretend they didn't know.
Woe be it in the city after the show,
If they missed the last train
Where would they go?

One dollar a night at the hotel to stay,
He would sneak in while she would pay.
The lamps were turned low, the hallways dark;
A warm bed was better than a bench in the park.

>(Citizens of Duffield
>Forgive me these tales.
>The truth bear out,
>The not guilty, shan't wail.)

>>uncle hank robison
>>the country poet

In every community there is that indispensable man. Perhaps, it is not fair to classify him with the obvious businesses but where would you put him? He cannot be overlooked. He is an institution without a degree but as close to a genius as he can be. He does something for about every family in the Duffield Community at least once a year. It might be major or minor, but he is there when needed. He will come to assistance at all hours of the night or on weekends. He never refuses especially if the job is a challenge. His talents are unlimited. He is a welder, blacksmith, plumber, machinist, carpenter, roofer, sheet-metal worker, brick and block layer, mason, farmer and conversationalist. He is a busy man, as perhaps you have already gathered. So busy, that he may not have time to repair the latch on his own back door, or buzz his own wood. He is a grandson of Benjamin Hillaker and highly regarded as Wayne Gilbert.

BUZZING WOOD WITH STEAM POWER
Buzzing wood at the Herrick place about 1900. The child with the little red wagon full of wood is Herb Herrick. Edward Herrick is second on the left. The twins, Edwin and Robert Herrick are second and first on the right. The engineer is in the background. Note water tank near the engine.

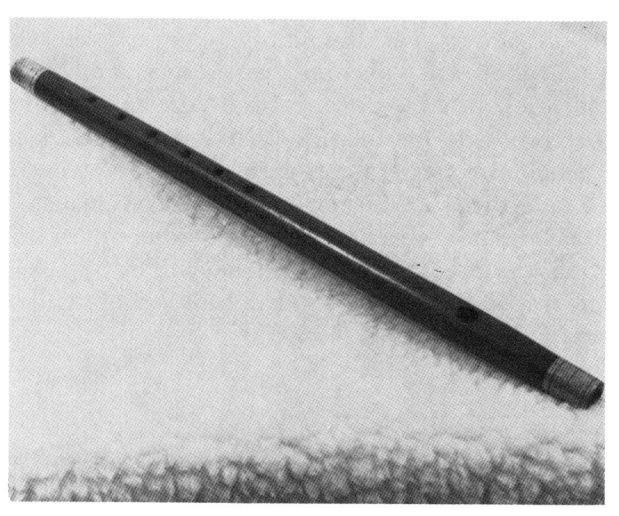

FIFE PLAYED IN THE WAR OF 1812
War of 1812 Fife played by Peter Perkins before he migrated to Michigan.

CHAPTER XI

PATRIOTS AND WAR VETERANS

As an historical preface for this chapter on War Veterans, special recognition is being given here to a few early American Patriots who were forefathers of people living in the Duffield Community.

Captain Archibald Dallas was a Revolutionary War Hero. He is seven generations removed from the children of John and Dorrine (Hendricks) Dallas who resided on Duffield Road near Hill Road. The Captain lost his life as he led his troops into a skirmish with the British on September 6, 1777 at Christianna Bridge in Delaware. This was five days before the Battle of Brandywine in which General Washington's Continentals were outflanked by General Howe's Army and forced to retreat to Philadelphia.

On September 3, 1901 a monument was dedicated at Christianna Bridge to mark the spot where the First Stars and Stripes was unfurled in a land battle. It was done by Captain Dallas just before he was shot down.

The Burton Family of Hill Road traces twice to the Putnams of the Revolutionary War.

General Israel Putnam's forces covered the retreat of the ragtag Continental Troops from Breed's Hill overlooking Boston Harbor on June 17, 1775. He ordered his men to fight Indian style. They were posted behind rail fences that were stuffed with hay and brush. The order given has become famous worldwide.

"Do not shoot until you can see the whites of their eyes." Defeat was turned into victory.

Rufus Putnam also fought at Boston. Later he commanded two regiments in the second Battle of Saratoga. He was a surveyor and laid out the original fortifications at West Point, a portion of which was named Fort Putnam. In 1787 he was a member of the Ohio Company and became its superintendent. Indian problems erupted in 1792 and he was appointed brigadier general with authority to solve them. He died in 1824 at the age of 86.

The situation with Peter Perkins is different from the trio previously mentioned, because he was an early settler in the area having been a member of the migration from Genesee County, New York in 1836. Peter was called a drummer boy in the War of 1812, but he played the fife. The instrument is retained by the family and is illustrated on page 138. He is also seven generations removed from the youth of this family that reside on Nichols and Miller Roads.

The fife players and drummers led the columns into the old stand-up style battles and were subject to extreme decimation. Somehow Peter Perkins was spared. He died March 3, 1881 at the age of 89 years, 9 months and 23 days.

DUFFIELD AREA WAR VETERANS

CIVIL WAR 1861-65

Brown, George W.	Harris, George K.	Smedley, Albert S.
Burton, James	Herrick, Norman	Van Vleet, Albert B.
Carrier, George	Kenyon, Francis	Whitmore, Francis
Davison, Rufus	Rall, Nathaniel W.	Whitmore, Milton
Derby, Charles	Ryno, Charles E.	

SPANISH AMERICAN WAR 1898-99

Baird, James

WORLD WAR I 1914-18

Blair, Frank J.	Hynes, Carl John	Kenyon, Howard R.
Blair, Gilbert H.	Hynes, Clement A.	O'Brien, Thomas
Chapman, George	Hynes, James	Potter, Kenneth
Craven, Frank L.	LaBarr, George N.	Sage, Elsworth A.
Gilmore, Frank	McCaughna, Howard	Warren, Joseph H.
Hardick, Jesse	Nimphie, Harlow C.	Wykes, Robert S.

Patriots And War Veterans

WORLD WAR II 1941-45

Atkinson, Emmett
Atkinson, William
Atkinson, Willis, Sr.
Beard, Harry
Bentley, Richard L.
Booth, Clarence I.
Buchanan, Lyle
Bush, Eugene T.
Bush, Howard H.
Cajka, Joseph
Chovanec, Stanley J.
Coffield, Floyd V.
Cowles, Francis
Dallas, Joseph L.
Delehanty, Lloyd
Dolehanty, Harold
Dolehanty, Paul
Drlik, Joseph P.
Eby, Evan E.
Edwards, Lawrence

Ellis, Donald
Ellis, Hoyt
Ferguson, A. J.
Gilbert, Wayne
Gurica, William
Hudy, George J., Sr.
Jancar, Steven
Jancar, John
Kanaar, Ralph
Lake, Lawrence W.
Liddie, Robert
Maul, Edward
McLaren, Lloyd R.
Middlesworth, Ray
Nechvil, Joseph K.
Nelson, Albert W.
Nimphie, Laverne
O'Brien, Edward
O'Brien, Richard
Perry, Vincent

Post, Edgar
Post, Harold
Porter, Kenneth G.
Potter, Lee
Purdy, Wayne
Reimel, Carl
Reimel, Floyd
Reimel, Louis
Reimel, Nelson H.
Reimel, Wilbur
Robison, Henry R.
Sonntag, Arthur F.
Sonntag, Jacquelyn
Tebby, William
Tinglan, Donald
Villerot, William E.
Warren, Gerald O.
Warren, John
Wheeler, Howard J.

KOREAN WAR 1950-53

Asplin, Wendell
Atkinson, Clyde
Atkinson, Gary
Bradley, Donald
Bush, Leland J.
Dallas, John D.
DeBarr, Kenneth E.

DeBarr, Louis J.
Delehanty, Daniel A.
Gooding, Harold J.
Hines, Frederick
Jenkins, Allen Dale
Lawrence, John
McBride, Aubrey A.

Parker, David A.
Post, Lynn
Rodgers, Virgil L.
Scheitler, Donald G.
Sedlarik, David C.
Suchy, Edward
Thwing, William J.

VIETNAM WAR 1964-73

Ackerman, Fred
Adams, Tracy
Atkinson, David
Atkinson, Steven
Atkinson, Willis Jr.
Austin, Donald
Bacon, Gregory R.
Chovanec, Gary

David, Larry J.
Gilbert, James
Gurica, Ted Allan
Hudy, George J. Jr.
Luna, Sherman L.
Morgan, Arnold
Morgan, Douglas
Morgan, Lawrence

Pittsley, Dan R.
Tandeske, Gordon D.
Trent, Monty G.
Waite, Randy L.
Wood, Gary L.
Woodard, Gary D.
Woodard, J. Lynn

TODAY'S BEDROOM COMMUNITY SOUTH OF HILL ROAD

Home in foreground is that of Donald and Helene Sloan, 6061 North Duffield Road, followed by home of Daniel and Doris Wilson, 6015 North Duffield, and that of Peter and Bette Dale, 6041 North Duffield.

TODAY'S BEDROOM COMMUNITY NORTH OF HILL ROAD

Brick home of Vernon and Carol DuPraw, 5486 North Duffield Road. Next is home of Albert and Linda Godley, 5498 North Duffield and in background is home of Morris and Mildred Taylor, 5510 North Duffield.

CHAPTER XII

CONCLUSION

IN SUMMATION one has to concede that Duffield has changed. It has not achieved the status of a ghost town as hundreds of lumbering and mining settlements have but it has ceased to exist as a commercial town. At this writing it is classified as a bedroom community.

The reason for this change is manyfold. Some of the obvious influences tend to be associated with the mobility of people and a change in their marketing habits. The desire of affluent people to own a home in the country has been stimulated by an "everybody is doing it" attitude. Some of the individual factors are: less pollution, less noise and crime, more space to raise a family, for relaxation and for enjoying friendly neighbors. This association of people seeking the good life is a quality that has been retained and is available within the modern Duffield Community. The visible proof is that all the lots or parcels of land that have been offered for sale have been purchased readily.

Duffield held all the ingredients necessary to become a ghost town, to disappear into oblivion, but it did not go over the brink. There ceased to be a need for a horse and buggy type supply of food and merchandise. The supply of clay for brick and tile manufacture was exhausted. The interest in the Golden Rod Arbor of the Gleaners waned. The blacksmith passed away. The elevator closed because good roads encouraged farmers to sell direct to terminal markets. Sugar beets were hauled direct to the refinery by truck. George Martin, the last Grand Trunk Western Depot Agent, was retired in 1931 and they locked the door. The railroad siding that serviced the sugar beet companies, the hay shed and the stockyard suffered a like fate each in its own way—so the trains did not stop anymore.

In spite of all of these reversals Duffield did not become a ghost town per se. Important counterbalances acted as equalizers. At least three equalizers have held the line.

The increase in population and the quality of the population that has made this modern bedroom community, is the first of these equalizers. The 1880 Census of Gaines Township was 1782 people. There are 3379 souls listed in the recent 1980 Census. There is no logical reason to conclude that the Duffield Corner of Gaines Township deviates from this 90% increase in population to any great extent. The exodus has been to the Duffield kind of country.

Agriculture has ceased to be the family venture, but it remains preponderate and is the second equalizer. It has become specialized. A handful of skilled men with costly machines now cultivate large fields where formerly this same soil was turned and gleaned in small fields by a multitude of workers. The Duffield Community has kept pace in agriculture as well as in the above population transition. Only 3% of our people are employed in the production of food and fiber, yet we are the best fed nation in the world and still able to consistently export over one third of our annual production to others who are in need.

There is more waste land than formerly. Highway right-of-ways have made wide slashes in rich soil that is returning to the primitive state. Governmental agencies are unable to convert them into parkways as planned. Likewise, land that has been sold off from prime farms in parcels from one to ten acres, for housing, is suffering. A few suburbanites will struggle with the soil for a couple of years but soon tire of the stoop labor it requires to maintain a large garden or to set it out to specialized cash crops such as strawberries, raspberries, asparagus, etc. Their burdensome dream space soon becomes an oversized lawn or it is returned to the primitive state. Much encouragement is

A DUFFIELD LANDMARK

This Dale Jenkins Family Home in Duffield tells it all better than words. This family is representative of the life-style that Duffield cherishes.

This structure, or portions thereof, has sheltered in turn, the George L. Carriers, Henry L. Nimphies and the Paul Drliks previous to the Jenkins family.

being tendered by the Soil Conservation Service toward reforestation of these areas. New woodlands that are established with desirable trees are not wastelands. They are the most valuable of renewable natural resources. If the shoe fits, look into good trees.

The most visible counterbalance that has saved the Duffield Community from being blotted out is the Rock.

So there you have the same three as in the beginning, when the first roots were firmly attached. To review they are: the indomitable spirit of the people who have matured from a sprinkling of hardy pioneers to the present inhabitants of this bedroom community, the stability of agriculture both as an economic factor and a way of life, and the Rock. All three have withstood the erosion of changing times.

Oh! Pardon me. I am always taking too much for granted. That is a very good question that you have asked.

The Rock is the Duffield Church.

> O, sometimes how long seems the day,
> And sometimes how weary my feet;
> But toiling, in life's dusty way,
> The Rock's blessed shadow, how sweet!
> O, then to the Rock let me fly,
> To the Rock that is higher than I.
>
>   Rock of Refuge
>   Erastus Johnson 1826-1909
>
> Copyrighted 1932
> The Methodist Book Concern

It is hoped, in the future that whenever you are asked by a stranger where you live, where you go to church, where you went to the old one room country school, where you spent many happy days, where your roots are or a location you have adopted because you just like the community, or any combination of these circumstances, you can reply confidently "We're from Duffield."

During the past fifty years inquisitors have always found it expedient to ask the second question, "Where is Duffield?"—and rightfully so.

We pray that these ramblings will be so widely read and passed about that never again will anyone be asked this discomforting question.

BIBLIOGRAPHY

History of Genesee County, Everts & Abbott 1879
History of Genesee County, Edwin O. Wood 1916
When Railroad was King, Frank N. Elliott 1961
One Hundred Years of Parke Davis & Company
Official Records of Duffield Methodist Church
Grand Trunk Reporter, November 1978
Gaines Area Centennial Booklet 1975
Court Records of Shiawassee County

Notes